FaithWeaver™
Children's
Messages 3

Group
Loveland, Colorado

D0052373

Group's R.E.A.L. Guarantee to you:

Every Group resource incorporates our R.E.A.L. approach to ministry—
a unique philosophy that results in long-term retention and life
transformation. It's ministry that's:

**This is EARL.
He's R.E.A.L.
mixed up.
(Get it?)**

Relational
Because student-to-
student interaction
enhances learning and
builds Christian
friendships.

Experiential
Because what students
experience sticks with
them up to 9 times
longer than what they
simply hear or read.

Applicable
Because the aim of
Christian education is
to be both hearers and
doers of the Word.

Learner-based
Because students learn
more and retain it
longer when the
process is designed
according to how they
learn best.

FaithWeaver™ Children's Messages 3
Copyright © 2001 Group Publishing, Inc.

Visit our Web site: **www.grouppublishing.com**

Credits

Contributing Authors: Cindy S. Hansen, Carol Mader, W.F. Meiklejohn, Shelby Mustain, Siv M.
Ricketts, Elaine Ernst Schneider, Donna Simcoe, Courtney Jennings Wright
Editor: Julie Meiklejohn
In-House Editor: Linda A. Anderson
Quality Control Editor: Dave Thornton
Chief Creative Officer: Joani Schultz
Copy Editor: Dena Twinem
Art Director: Kari K. Monson
Cover Art Director/Designer: Lisa Chandler
Computer Graphic Artist: Shelly Dillon
Cover Photographer: Bohm/Marrazzo
Illustrator: Jan Knudson
Production Manager: Peggy Naylor

ISBN: 0-7644-2336-3

10 9 8 7 6 5 4 3 2 1   10 09 08 07 06 05 04 03 02 01

Printed in the United States of America.

Contents

Introduction

Welcome to the third book in the FaithWeaver™ Children's Messages series. These are not your everyday, ordinary children's messages. Instead of having children sit and listen passively to what amounts to an abbreviated version of an adult sermon, these messages engage kids, surprise them, and draw them into spiritual growth. Your children will not only have fun, but will walk away with a deeper understanding of how Bible stories apply to their lives.

Each message in *FaithWeaver™ Children's Messages 3* explores one Bible story, helping children to experience what happened to the people in the story. These experiences lead children to understand a Bible verse that contains a core biblical truth. For example, kids will use a magnet to learn, as Solomon did, that we should always turn to God. This kind of active learning makes sense to children, and therefore cements biblical truths in their hearts.

All of your children will look forward to hearing the children's message every week. The messages appeal to children from preschool age through elementary-school age. Be sure to attend to the special needs of younger students during your children's message time, and encourage older students to help younger ones with the activities. You can also involve your other congregation members, who will be refreshed by new perspectives from these messages—and from the children! You may use a microphone or repeat what children say, hold up props so that congregation members can experience the stories as kids do, and even encourage your congregation to cheer or sing along with the kids. These Bible-based children's messages will touch both children's and adults' lives.

We've arranged *FaithWeaver Children's Messages 3* to parallel the four quarters (fall, winter, spring, summer) that most churches use for Sunday school and other educational programs. The book contains four sections of thirteen sermons—one sermon a week for an entire year. The fall quarter begins with David being crowned king of the Israelites and follows the Israelites through the division of the kingdom. For the winter and spring quarters, we cover the New Testament stories of Jesus' birth, life, death, and resurrection so children can focus on Christ during Christmas and Easter. Then the summer quarter returns to the Old Testament and the adventures of Bible heroes such as Jonah, Daniel, and Job.

Use the messages in the order suggested here, rearrange them to coincide with holidays or events, or choose Bible stories and verses that fit your own themes. The Bible stories listed in the table of contents and the Scripture index will help you choose the Bible stories and Scriptures you want to teach.

You can also use this book in conjunction with Group's FaithWeaver™ curriculum for fall 2001 through summer 2002, is available from your local Christian bookstore or Group Publishing. Using *FaithWeaver Children's Messages 3* along with this family ministry curriculum helps you reinforce Bible stories and verses in a way that cements Bible truths in kids' lives.

SECTION
ONE

FALL
QUARTER

David Becomes King

Bible Story: 2 Samuel 5:1-5; Psalm 37

Bible Verse: "God is our refuge and strength, an ever-present help in trouble" (Psalm 46:1).

Simple Supplies: *You'll need a Bible, a paper crown, envelopes, Christian stickers, and individually wrapped pieces of candy. Before the message, put several stickers and a piece of candy in each of several envelopes and seal the envelopes. You'll need one envelope for each child.*

ive each child a sealed envelope. I've given each of you a special envelope. Don't open it until I tell you to. For now, I'd like you to put it on the floor behind your back. *Pause.* What do you think is inside the envelopes? *Pause.* You'll have to wait for a little while and then you'll find out what's in the envelopes.

Hold up the paper crown. Who can tell me what this is? *Pause for responses.* Who would wear a crown? *Pause for responses.* Today we're going to talk about a man named David who became a king. David had to wait a long time before he got to become king. Have you ever had to wait a long time for something? *Pause for responses.* How did it feel to wait? Was it easy or hard? *Pause for responses.* How do you think David felt about waiting? *Pause.*

David was just a teenager when he found out that God had chosen him to be king. How would you feel if you found out right now that you were going to be a king or queen when you grew up? *Pause.* David was not worried or nervous or even impatient because he knew that God would take care of him. As David grew older, Saul, the man who was already king, got very jealous of David. What does it mean to be jealous? *Pause.* Saul got so jealous and angry with David that he wanted to kill him. David even had to hide from Saul so Saul wouldn't hurt him.

After several years, King Saul died in a battle with the Philistines, and David finally became king. All this time, David had waited patiently for his turn to be king. David knew that God would keep him safe from Saul and give him the strength to wait until it was his turn to be king.

Open your Bible to Psalm 46:1, and show the page to the children.

Psalm 46:1 says, **"God is our refuge and strength, an ever-present help in trouble."** What do you think a refuge is? *Pause.* A refuge is like a place of safety. God will always take care of us in hard times. We can also depend on God for patience. What's something you've needed God's help to wait for? *Pause for responses.* Have you had times when you've been afraid? Tell me about them. *Pause for responses.* The next time you're scared or having trouble waiting for something, you can ask God to give you patience. Do you think you can remember to do that? *Wait for children to respond.* All you have to do is ask him. You can always depend on God to take care of you.

David was very patient. He knew that he could count on God to keep him safe from Saul. David also counted on God for the strength to help him to wait until it was his turn to be king. You've also had to wait for something today. Has it been hard to wait to open your envelopes? *Pause.* You haven't had to wait as long as David had to wait to be king, but you have had to be patient. I'm going to ask you to wait a little longer. I want you to wait until you go back to your seats to open your envelopes and find out what's inside. Can you wait a few more minutes? *Pause.*

Let's thank God for helping us to be patient and to wait. Dear God, thank you for helping us wait for our turn. Help us to be patient while we wait. Thank you for loving us and always watching over us. In Jesus' name, amen.

As you open your envelopes, remember that the next time you have to wait for something, you can ask God to help you be patient.

David Is Merciful to Mephibosheth

Bible Story: 2 Samuel 9:1-13

> **Bible Verse:** "Be devoted to one another in brotherly love. Honor one another above yourselves" (Romans 12:10).

Simple Supplies: *You'll need a Bible, paper bowls, plastic spoons, napkins, a large pot, and a large spoon or ladle.*

As children come forward, hand each child a paper napkin, a plastic spoon, and a paper bowl. Have children sit around you and direct them to spread their napkins on their laps as if they are preparing to eat a meal. Hey, kids! We're going to pretend we're about to eat. I've got my cooking bowl and a big spoon. I'll be the cook. What would you like me to cook for you? *Pause for responses.* Those all sound like great things to eat! I'll have to think about what groceries I will need to cook those dishes. Then I will need to go to the store and buy the ingredients. And I'll have to have the money to pay for the food I buy at the grocery store. After that, I'll have to plan when I'll have the time to cook it all. Whew! That's a lot to think about. Who does the meal planning and grocery shopping at your house? *Pause. Allow children to comment.* Who cooks the meals? *Pause. Allow children to answer.*

Mephibosheth was a person who lived in Bible days. He was the grandson of King Saul. When Mephibosheth was a little boy, he lived in the palace, and he never had to worry about food or clothing. But King Saul died, and Mephibosheth didn't live in the palace anymore. It was hard for him to take care of himself because he had two crippled feet. King David heard about Mephibosheth, and he asked him to come to the palace. Mephibosheth may have been afraid to see King

David. Many years before, when Mephibosheth's grandfather Saul was the king of Israel, Saul was mean to David. Maybe Mephibosheth was scared that King David would be angry with him because of what his grandfather had done.

When Mephibosheth arrived at the royal palace, King David greeted him warmly. Perhaps he shook his hand. Can you shake your neighbor's hand? *Pause.* He may have even hugged Mephibosheth. Can you hug someone near you? *Pause.* David told Mephibosheth that he had been a friend of his father, Jonathan. Jonathan was King Saul's son. And now King David wanted to be kind to Jonathan's son, Mephibosheth.

King David told Mephibosheth that he would never have to worry about having something to eat again. *Pretend to ladle food from the big pot into each child's paper bowl.* Just as I'm pretending to fill your bowls right now, King David promised that he would make sure Mephibosheth's bowl was always full. King David invited Mephibosheth to eat with him at his table at the palace and to be just like his own son. David wanted to show the kindness of God to Mephibosheth.

We can show God's kindness too. Can you use your spoon to put pretend food in your friend's bowl? *Pause.* Can someone put some food in my bowl? *Pause.* How about that lady in the first row? Can someone take a bowl to her and pretend to spoon some food from your bowl to hers? *Pause.* God wants us to show his kindness to others, just as David was kind to Mephibosheth. Can you think of someone who might need food? What could you do to help? *Pause for children to respond.*

 Open your Bible to Romans 12:10, and show the page to the children. Romans 12:10 says, **"Be devoted to one another in brotherly love. Honor one another above yourselves."** In this verse, God is instructing us to be kind. God says that we should treat one another in brotherly love, which means that he wants us to treat each other like family. King David treated Mephibosheth like he was his son. He treated him like family. King David showed God's kindness to Mephibosheth. *Lead kids in prayer.*

 Dear God, thank you for the example of King David and Mephibosheth. Help us to learn from this story how to be kind and how to help others. In Jesus' name, amen.

Don't forget to take your napkins, bowls, and spoons with you. When you look at them, think about how Mephibosheth's bowl was always full because King David showed the kindness of God.

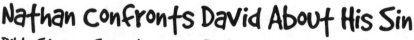

Nathan Confronts David About His Sin

Bible Story: 2 Samuel 11:1–12:10; Psalm 51:1–12

Bible Verse: "If we confess our sins, he is faithful and just and will forgive us our sins and purify us from all unrighteousness" (1 John 1:9).

Simple Supplies: *You'll need a Bible, marshmallows, and resealable plastic bags. Put one marshmallow in each of several bags and five marshmallows in each of several bags.*

Have you ever done anything wrong? Have you ever seen someone else do something wrong? *Pause for children to respond.*

Today we'll hear about a man who did something wrong and had another man tell him he needed to admit his wrongdoing.

Our story today is about King David. One day, King David was walking on his roof, and he saw a beautiful woman. The woman's name was Bathsheba. David decided that he wanted Bathsheba to be his wife, but she was already married to a man named Uriah. So David did a very bad thing. He sent Uriah into a battle so that he would die. Why is it wrong to hurt someone else to get something you really want? *Pause.*

In today's story, another man was brave enough to tell David what he had done wrong. That man was named Nathan. Nathan was a prophet, and God had told him what David did. So Nathan told David a story.

Have children form trios. Give one child in each trio a bag with one marshmallow. Give another child in the trio a bag with five marshmallows, and don't give any marshmallows to the third child. Tell children it's very important not to eat their marshmallows yet.

The story Nathan told was about a poor man who had one little lamb. The lamb was very special to this man, and he treated the lamb as if it was a member of his family. The lamb ate and slept with his family. The man loved the lamb. *Have children holding just one marshmallow hold it up.*

There was another man who was very rich, and he had many lambs. *Have children holding the five marshmallows lift them up.* The rich man had a guest come to visit him one day. *Have the children with no marshmallows wave at the children with five marshmallows as though they're saying "hello."*

What do you think the rich man served his guest for dinner? *Pause.* The rich man took the one little lamb of the poor man to serve to his guest! *Have children with five marshmallows take the one marshmallow from their partners. Then have the children with five marshmallows give one marshmallow to the "guest." Again, tell kids not to eat the marshmallows yet.*

Do you think what the rich man did was fair? Why or why not? *Pause.*

Well, when David heard this story, he became very angry. He didn't think what the rich man did was fair. Then Nathan told David, "You are the man!" David admitted that he had been wrong and told God that he was sorry. What do you think God did when David confessed? *Pause.* God forgave him! Isn't that wonderful? Our Bible verse for today tells us about God's forgiveness. Let's take a look at it. But first, let's share all of our marshmallows with each other. *Have children open the bags and share all of the marshmallows so that each child has two.*

Open your Bible to 1 John 1:9, and show the page to the children. 1 John 1:9 says, **"If we confess our sins, he is faithful and just and will forgive us our sins and purify us from all unrighteousness."**

What does "confess" mean? *Pause.* Confess means to admit to God that you've done something wrong. How many of you have never done anything wrong? *Pause.* The Bible tells us that Jesus is the only one who never did anything wrong. What does that mean we need to do? *Pause.* It means we all need to confess at one time or another. What does God do when we confess? He forgives us, just as he forgave David! Let's pray right now and ask God to forgive us for anything you can think of that you've done wrong. It can be anything, such as disobeying your parents, being mean to your little sister or brother, or not doing your homework. *Lead kids in prayer.*

Dear God, please forgive us for the things we've done wrong. Thank you that your Word promises that you'll forgive us. Help us to always be willing to admit when we've done something wrong and confess our sins. In Jesus' name, amen.

Absalom Rebels and Is Defeated

Bible Story: 2 Samuel 15:1-12; 17:1-12; 18:1-18

Bible Verse: "He has showed you, O man, what is good. And what does the Lord require of you? To act justly and to love mercy and to walk humbly with your God"(Micah 6:8).

Simple Supplies: *You'll need a Bible, a large forked branch, a marker, and a piece of poster board. Write the words of the Bible verse on the poster board.*

What do you think God wants you to do? *Pause.* That's what a man named Micah wondered when he wrote this verse. *Show children the Bible verse written on the poster board and read it aloud together.* "To act justly" means to be fair. "To love mercy" means to be kind, and "to walk humbly" means

to let God be in charge every day. Let's stand up and make some motions together to help us remember this verse. **He** *(point up to God)* **has showed you, O man** *(point outward)*, **what is good. And what does the Lord require of you?** *(Hold your palms up as if you're asking a question.)* **To act justly** *(pretend to place a crown on your head)* **and to love mercy** *(stretch out your arms in front of you)* **and to walk** *(walk in place)* **humbly with your God.**

Open your Bible to 2 Samuel 15, and show the page to the children. Have the kids stand so they can act out the motions. David was a good king who acted justly. *(Pretend to place a crown on your head.)* He loved mercy *(stretch out your arms in front of you)* and he walked humbly *(walk in place)* with his God. Unfortunately, his son grew into a man who didn't act justly, who didn't love mercy, and who didn't walk with God. David's son's name was Absalom. Everyone noticed Absalom. In fact, he even had a statue made of himself. Absalom decided that he wanted to be the king of Israel instead of his father David. So he came up with a sneaky plan to steal the throne and the crown.

Absalom gave himself a fancy chariot and made fifty men run ahead of him so everyone would think he was important. Absalom kissed people's hands and told them what a wonderful leader he would make. When the people came to talk to King David, Absalom would get to them first. This is how he stole the hearts of the Israelites. Finally Absalom sent out secret messengers with trumpets to blow announcing that he was the new king. When King David heard about it, he said, "Oh, no, we must run or none of us will escape the sword of Absalom!" So King David and his followers escaped into the desert.

Absalom moved into the palace. One of Absalom's helpers told him to chase after David and kill him. Absalom rubbed his hands together and said, "This sounds like a good plan." Now, is that any way to act justly *(pretend to place a crown on your head)*, love mercy *(stretch out your arms)*, and to walk humbly *(walk in place)* with your God? No!

Another leader said, "Don't do that. David is a fierce fighter, as wild as a bear robbed of her cubs. He's smart, too. David is probably hiding in a cave. Don't just go after David. Go after his entire army. Attack them until no one is left alive."

Absalom said, "Hmm, this plan is even better!" Now, is that any way to act justly *(pretend to place a crown on your head)*, love mercy *(stretch out your arms)*, and to walk humbly *(walk in place)* with your God? No way!

David heard about the plan. He got his army together, and David's troops marched into the field to fight against the troops of his very own son. The battle was a long, tough one, and many men died. In the end, King David and his troops emerged the winners.

Hold up the branch vertically. We have two roads we can walk in life. *Trace one branch in one direction.* We can act justly *(crown on head)* and love mercy *(reach out your arms)* and walk humbly *(walk in place)* with our God, as David did. *Trace the other branch.* Or we can be greedy and live only for ourselves, like Absalom. *Hold out the branch.* The greedy grabbing Absalom got grabbed in the end. Can you tell me some ways to act justly? to love mercy? How can you walk humbly with your God? *Pause. Break off a piece of the branch for each child, and ask the kids to take them home as reminders to follow the path of justice, mercy, and walking humbly with God.*

Let's say the verse one more time together, and then I'll pray it. **He** *(point up to God)* **has showed you, O man** *(point outward)*, **what is good. And what does the Lord require of you?** *(Hold your palms up as if you're asking a question.)* **To act justly** *(pretend to place a crown on your head)* **and to love mercy** *(stretch out your arms in front of you)* **and to walk** *(walk in place)* **humbly with your God.** *Lead kids in prayer.*

You have showed us, O Lord, what is good and what you require of us. You ask us to act justly and to love mercy and to walk humbly with you, our God. Help us to choose the best path for our lives. Help us to walk humbly with you throughout our lives. In Jesus' name, amen.

Solomon Rules Wisely

Bible Story: 1 Kings 2:1-4; 3:3-28

Bible Verse: "If any of you lacks wisdom, he should ask God, who gives generously to all without finding fault, and it will be given to him" (James 1:5).

Simple Supplies: *You'll need a Bible, three different kinds of snacks, three bowls, and small cups. Put one kind of snack in each bowl. You'll need enough for each child to have a small helping of each snack.*

What does it mean to be wise? How do you think a person gets to be wise? Who is the wisest person you know? Why do you think that person is wise? *Pause for children to respond after each question.* Being wise is more than just being smart; when a person is wise, he or she knows how to use that intelligence in the best way possible. That person can use his or her intelligence to make the best decisions in any situation.

Today we'll learn about the wisest man in the Bible, Solomon. Solomon was David's son. Before David died, he gave Solomon some very good advice. He told Solomon to always obey God and do what God told him to do.

How many of you always do what's right? *Pause.* Is it always easy to do what's right? Why or why not? *Pause.* What do you think you would need in order to help you always know the right thing to do? *Pause.*

If you could ask for anything you wanted from God, what would you ask for? *Pause.*

Take out the snacks you've brought for the children, and give each child a small cup. I have some yummy snacks here that I'd like to share with you. Take a look at the snacks and decide which kind you'd like. *Take a quick poll of some of the kids and ask them which snack they'll choose. Then go to each child, one at a time, and ask him or her which kind of snack he or she would like. Then pour a little of each of the snacks in his or her cup. Tell kids they can eat the snacks.*

Just as you asked for only one of these snacks and were given all three, Solomon was given a chance to ask God for anything he wanted. Solomon knew just what to ask for! Let's find out what that was.

Open your Bible to 1 Kings 3:7-9, and read the passage aloud.

Solomon asked God for wisdom. What do you think God's answer was? Let's read on and find out. *Read 1 Kings 3:10-12 aloud.*

Wow! Not only did God give Solomon what he asked for—wisdom—but God also gave Solomon all the things he could have asked for but didn't. Solomon was also given riches, honor, and a promise for a long life as long as Solomon always followed God's ways. God gave Solomon these things because he was so pleased with Solomon's earnest request for wisdom.

Our Bible verse today tells us how we can get wisdom too. Let's read it together. *Open your Bible to James 1:5, and show the page to the children.* James 1:5 says, **"If any of you lacks wisdom, he should ask God, who gives generously to all without finding fault, and it will be given to him."**

Let's pray right now and ask God to give us wisdom to know how to always do what's right. *Lead children in prayer.*

Dear God, please give us wisdom so that we will know to do what is right. Thank you that you give us wisdom when we ask for it. In Jesus' name, amen.

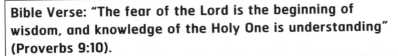

Solomon Writes Many Proverbs

Bible Story: 1 Kings 4:29-34; Proverbs 1:1-7

> **Bible Verse:** "The fear of the Lord is the beginning of wisdom, and knowledge of the Holy One is understanding" (Proverbs 9:10).

Simple Supplies*: You'll need a Bible, masking tape, a marker, and two pieces of paper. Create two paths on the floor with the masking tape. They'll need to be fairly close to each other. Write "Bad, Foolish Path" on one piece of paper and "Good, Wise Path" on the other piece. Tape one sign near each path.*

Point out the two paths to children. As you grow up, you'll be choosing a path to take through life. Both paths may look good, but one path is a better choice than the other one. *Point to the "Bad, Foolish Path."* When you take the bad, foolish path, you will make wrong choices. You might hurt other people. You might do wrong things, and you may hurt yourself. You might waste your time, your money, and your talents, and you may not feel good about yourself. God will be sad about the choices you make on the bad path. What are some bad paths people sometimes choose to follow? *Pause for responses.*

Point to the "Good, Wise Path." If you take the good path of wisdom, you'll have a more peace-filled life. You will be happy with the person you are. You will have true, loving friends, and you'll develop your abilities. Your life will make others happy too. And, most important, God will be pleased. What are some good paths people choose to follow? *Pause for responses.*

Which path would you choose—the good path of wisdom or the bad path of foolishness? *Pause.* The paths in our lives aren't usually as well-marked as these two paths are—how will you know the difference? *Lay down your Bible in front of the good path.* God doesn't trick us or let us wonder which is the wisest path to take. *Have an older child open the Bible to 1 Kings 4:29–34, and show the page to the children.*

This story is about a man named Solomon. God gave Solomon wisdom. What is wisdom? *Pause.* Wisdom is being able to tell the right path from the wrong path, and then doing what's right. You can be smart and know a lot of things, but only people who are wise will do the right things. If you ask God for wisdom, he will help you to choose the right path. God said he would give Solomon whatever he wanted, and Solomon asked for wisdom. King Solomon said, "Help me to know the difference between right and wrong."

Oh, how God loved that prayer! And how God answered that prayer. God gave Solomon wisdom and understanding as measureless as the sand on the seashore. Solomon spoke three thousand proverbs. What Solomon wrote are words of understanding for living a smart life and for doing what is right and fair. Solomon said it best when he said that the fear, or respect, of the Lord is the beginning of being wise. Only fools choose to ignore God.

Solomon became so famous for being wise that people from all nations came to listen to his wisdom. Wouldn't it have been great to have met this man?

We don't have to travel to Israel, or back in time, to hear Solomon's wisdom. Where can we get it? *Pause.* That's right. *Show children the book of Proverbs in your Bible.* We only have to open our Bibles to get wisdom. The book of Proverbs is a collection of little pieces of Solomon's wisdom that we can read every day. Many of Solomon's proverbs start by telling what happens when we follow the bad path and then go on to say what will happen if we choose the good path. I'm going to read a few of Solomon's proverbs to you now. For each one, I'd like you to start by standing on the bad, foolish path. When you hear me saying what happens on the good path, I'd like you to jump onto the good path of wisdom.

Proverbs 10:19 says when you talk too much, you are going to sin. He who holds his tongue is wise. *Pause to allow children to jump onto the good path.* What do you think this proverb means? *Pause for responses.*

Have children jump back onto the bad path. Here's another one. Proverbs 11:1 says the Lord hates it when people are dishonest and try to cheat to get extra money. But people who are honest are his delight. *Pause to allow children to jump onto the good path.* What do you think this proverb means? *Pause for responses.*

16

Have children jump back onto the bad path. How about one more? Proverbs 11:13 says a gossip tells other people's secrets. A trustworthy man keeps a secret. *Pause to allow children to jump onto the good path.* What do you think this proverb means? *Pause for responses.*

The entire book of Proverbs is packed with these yummy nuggets of truth and wisdom to help you to live a wise, happy life. Read it for yourself!

Proverbs 9:10 says, **"The fear of the Lord is the beginning of wisdom, and knowledge of the Holy One is understanding."** This verse tells us that when we get to know God and his ways better, we will become wise. How can we get to know God better? *Pause for responses.* We can spend time with God by praying and reading about his wisdom in the Bible. We can ask God for wisdom and under-standing, just like Solomon did. *Lead kids in prayer.*

Dear God, as we make our way through life, help us each to choose the path which pleases you. Help us to ask for wisdom like Solomon did. Help us turn to your Word to help us choose the right path and stay on it throughout our lives. In Jesus' name, amen.

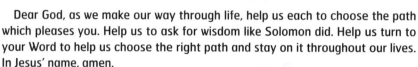

Solomon Turns Away from God

Bible Story: 1 Kings 11:1-13

> **Bible Verse:** "Trust in the Lord with all your heart and lean not on your own understanding; in all your ways acknowledge him, and he will make your paths straight" (Proverbs 3:5-6).

Simple Supplies: *You'll need a Bible, a magnet with a plastic handle, and paper clips.*

S *how the magnet to the children.* What is this? *Pause for children to respond.* Yes, it's a magnet. What does a magnet do? *Pause.* A magnet attracts metal, doesn't it? *Pass out the paper clips to the children.* I'm going to let each of you take a turn using the magnet. *Let each child have a turn attracting a paper clip to the magnet.* What would happen if we turned the magnet around? *Show the children the plastic handle of the magnet.* Would this part of the magnet attract the metal? *Pause for children to respond. Pass the magnet around again and let the children try to attract the paper clips with the plastic end of the magnet.* Could the plastic end attract the metal? *Pause.* Only the magnet part could attract the metal, couldn't it? When we turned it away, we couldn't attract the metal anymore. It just wouldn't work right. It's the same way for us and our relationships with God. When we turn away from God, things in our lives just don't work right either.

A man named Solomon turned away from God. Have you heard of Solomon? *Pause for children to respond.* Solomon was David's son, and he became the king of Israel. Solomon had a wise heart, and he loved God. One day God told Solomon that he didn't want him to marry any women from other nations. God had told all of the people of Israel not to marry women from other nations because they worshipped different gods instead of our God, the one, true God.

Do you think Solomon listened to God? *Pause.* No, Solomon did not listen to God. He married those women from other nations who worshipped other gods. They turned Solomon's heart away from God. When Solomon turned away from God, things in his life didn't work right, just like when we turned the magnet away from the paper clips. Do you think God was happy with Solomon? *Pause for children to respond.* God was very angry with Solomon. He told Solomon that he would be punished for turning away. God would take away most of the kingdom from Solomon's son, and he would only get to be king of a small part. Does God like it when we turn away from him? *Pause.*

Open your Bible to Proverbs 3:5-6, and show the page to the children.

Proverbs 3:5-6 says, **"Trust in the Lord with all your heart and lean not on your own understanding; in all your ways acknowledge him, and he will make your paths straight."** Can you remember a time when you had a decision or a choice to make? *Pause for children to respond.* How did you make the decision? Did you ask anyone for help or get anyone's advice while you were trying to make the decision? *Pause for children to respond.* Our Bible verse tells us to trust God. One way to trust God is to turn to him, just as we turned the magnet around to attract the metal. If we keep our lives focused on God by reading the Bible, going to church and Sunday school, and spending time in prayer, then God will help us follow in his footsteps. Then he will make our "paths straight."

Take out the magnet and a paper clip. Turn the plastic handle toward the paper clip. When we turn away from God, things don't work right. *Switch the magnet around and let it attract the paper clip.* Once we decide to turn back toward God, he's right there waiting for us. We make God sad when we turn away from him, but he never leaves us.

Let's thank God for never turning away from us. Dear God, thank you for never turning away from us. We know that if we trust in you, you'll direct our paths. Help us to follow you each day. In Jesus' name, amen.

The Kingdom Divides

Bible Story: 1 Kings 11:28–12:24

> **Bible Verse:** "If my people, who are called by my name, will humble themselves and pray and seek my face and turn from their wicked ways, then will I hear from heaven and will forgive their sin and will heal their land" (2 Chronicles 7:14).

Simple Supplies: *You'll need a Bible, construction paper, clear self-adhesive shelf paper, and an artist's rendition of God (if you can't find a picture of God, write "God" in big letters on one sheet of construction paper). Cut several 6x4-inch strips of the shelf paper, enough for each child to have one. Hide the picture of God somewhere in your worship area.*

Today we're going to talk about rebellion. Who can tell me what it means to rebel? *Pause for children to answer.* Rebellion means to disobey even when you know something is wrong. It means you don't listen to people you are supposed to listen to, like your parents, teachers, policemen, and God.

There are two men in today's Bible story: Jeroboam, who did what God wanted, and Rehoboam, who rebelled against God. Let's find out what happened to them.

Open your Bible to 1 Kings 11:28–12:24, and show the passage to the children.

Jeroboam was one of King Solomon's important men. He was put in charge of all the workers. One day, a prophet named Ahijah met Jeroboam on the road when he was on his way to Israel. He told Jeroboam about God's plan for Israel. *Give each child a piece of construction paper.*

Ahijah took his coat and tore it into twelve pieces. *Have children tear their pieces of construction paper into twelve pieces.* Ahijah told Jeroboam that the twelve pieces represented twelve kingdoms and that Jeroboam was going to be king over ten of those kingdoms. *Have each child keep ten of his or her pieces, and collect the other pieces.*

Solomon was king at this time, but he had started to do things his own way instead of God's way. Because of this, God decided to leave only two kingdoms for Solomon's son, Rehoboam, to rule. But all the other kingdoms were to be ruled by Jeroboam, the man who was obeying God's ways.

When Solomon found out about this, he tried to kill Jeroboam. So Jeroboam ran away to Egypt. When Solomon died, the people of Israel wanted Jeroboam to come back, and he did. But by then Rehoboam had made himself king and was being cruel to the people.

When all the people heard that Jeroboam had returned, they sent for him and wanted to make him king. Rehoboam prepared for a battle to make sure he stayed king. But another prophet of God, who was a good prophet, told the men who were going to fight that God didn't want them to fight. God had planned for things to happen just the way they did. So the fighting men obeyed God's message and they didn't fight. Jeroboam became the new king, just as God had promised. *Have each child take the ten pieces of torn construction paper and place them on one-half of a piece of clear self-adhesive shelf paper and then fold the other half of the paper over the construction paper pieces.* You can take these home and use them as bookmarks to remind you of what God did for Jeroboam.

Our Bible verse today tells us what happens when we follow God's commands and stop rebelling against God. Let's read it. *Open your Bible to 2 Chronicles 7:14, and show the page to the children.* Second Chronicles 7:14 says, **"If my people, who are called by my name, will humble themselves and pray and seek my face and turn from their wicked ways, then will I hear from heaven and will forgive their sin and will heal their land."**

What does it mean to seek God's face? *Pause.*

Somewhere in this room, I've placed a picture of God. Now we all know that we can't really know what God looks like, so this is just a picture of what someone thinks God looks like. But I want you to try to find that picture of God's face. I will give you instructions that you must follow closely. If you don't follow my instructions, you won't find the picture.

Have children start looking for the picture you've hidden. Give them instructions such as, "Take ten steps forward, turn to your left, take three steps forward, turn to your right." The instructions you give should lead those following your instructions directly to the picture. Once children have found the picture, have them bring it to you.

How were you able to find the picture of God's face? *Pause.* Do you think you would have been able to find it if you hadn't followed my directions? Why or why not? *Pause.*

Our Bible verse tells us that not only are we supposed to seek God's face, but we are supposed to stop doing wrong things, too. One of those wrong things is rebellion. Let's pray right now and ask God to help us obey and not be rebellious. *Lead children in prayer.*

Dear God, please help us to always obey you and not be rebellious. Show us when we are starting to do things our own way instead of your way. In Jesus' name, amen.

Elijah Helps a Widow

Bible Story: 1 Kings 17:7-24

> **Bible Verse:** "So do not worry, saying, 'What shall we eat?' or 'What shall we drink?' or 'What shall we wear?' But seek first his kingdom and his righteousness, and all these things will be given to you as well" (Matthew 6:31, 33).

Simple Supplies: *You'll need a Bible, a large bowl, flour, and a piece of bread or a roll for each child. Put a small amount of flour in the bowl. Plan to have someone help you during this message. Gather the children near a podium or another piece of furniture that the helper can hide behind. Ask the helper to put rolls or bread in the bowl when you set it behind the podium.*

*S*how the children the flour in the bottom of the bowl. What can you make out of this much flour? Not much, right? You probably couldn't make anything to eat with only a tiny bit of flour. *Put the bowl behind the podium.* Have you ever been really hungry? *Pause.* Were you hungry for a long time, or just a little while? *Pause.* People in the land of Israel were hungry, thirsty, and scared. God had stopped any rain from falling on Israel because their king, King Ahab, had started to worship a fake god named Baal. God had warned the Israelites that if they worshipped idols, God would keep the rain from falling. Plants and animals died. There was nothing anyone could do but wait.

Elijah was a prophet from God. He brought God's word to the people. God told Elijah to go to a widow, a woman whose husband had died. After his long journey, Elijah found the widow and her son picking up sticks. The little boy's clothes hung on his skinny body. He looked hungry. Elijah was hungry too. Show me how you look when you feel hungry. *Pause for children's responses.* Elijah said to the widow, "Please bring me a piece of bread."

She looked at him. In a hollow voice, she said, "I don't have any bread—only a handful of flour and a little oil. I am gathering a few sticks to take home and make a meal for myself and my son, so that we can eat it—and die."

How would you feel if you had no food, no money, and no one to help you? *Pause.* That would be a pretty scary feeling, wouldn't it? But we never have to be afraid or worried. Jesus said, **"So do not worry, saying, 'What shall we eat?' or 'What shall we drink?' or 'What shall we wear?' But seek first his kingdom and his righteousness, and all these things will be given to you as well"** (Matthew 6:31, 33).

Elijah knew he could trust God. He told the woman, "Don't be afraid. Go home and make your cake of bread, one for me and one for you. For God has told me that your flour and oil will not run out."

The widow did as Elijah told her. She believed. And every day when she reached into her jar there was...flour! Food! Just as God had promised. The widow, Elijah, and the little boy had plenty of good bread to eat! *Pull out the bowl and act surprised to see the rolls which are now in it. Pass around the bowl and let each child take a roll or a piece of bread to munch on while you continue the story.* Elijah loved seeing the little boy get a little fatter and happier.

Guess what? Our good story gets better. But first, it gets sad. Some time later the little boy became sick. He grew weaker and weaker. One awful day, he stopped breathing. You can't live for more than a few minutes without air. The woman ran to Elijah with her son dangling in her arms. Show me how you look when you're really sad. *Pause for children's responses.*

Elijah simply took the boy from her arms and said, "Give me your son." He went into the house and laid the boy on his bed. Elijah cried out to the Lord. With all his heart and all his might and all of the faith he could use, Elijah stretched himself out and cried, "O Lord my God, let this boy's life return to him!" *Pause. Close your eyes.*

God heard Elijah's prayers and gave the little boy back his life! Elijah carried the boy back to his mother and said, "Look, your son is alive!" Elijah and the widow knew at that moment that God's words are true. Oh, how happy we are when God meets our needs!

What are some things you worry about? *Pause.* Do you know people who worry about what they will eat and wear? *Pause.* Jesus said we should not worry about what we will eat or drink or wear. He will give us all we need. You can think of yourself as a baby bird in the nest of Jesus' arms. He will feed you. He will protect you. He will take care of you. *Lead children in prayer.*

Dear God, thank you that we never have to worry about food or life. You promised us that you would take care of us when we take care of seeking you. In Jesus' name, amen.

Elijah Challenges the Prophets of Baal

Bible Story: 1 Kings 18:16-40

> **Bible Verse:** "I am the Lord your God, who brought you out of Egypt, out of the land of slavery. You shall have no other gods before me" (Exodus 20:2-3).

Simple Supplies: *You'll need a Bible and small twigs or sticks. Scatter the sticks around your children's message area.*

Have you ever called to someone and they didn't answer? *Pause and let the children respond.* How did that make you feel? *Pause and let the children respond.* How do you think you would feel if you tried all day long, shouting and dancing around, and there still was no answer? *Pause and let the children share their feelings.* It sounds like we would be sad, disappointed, and maybe even angry if we tried and tried to talk to someone and there was no answer.

A long time ago, there was a king who told everyone in the country that they had to believe in many different gods. A man named Elijah lived in that country, but he worshipped only God. This made the king angry. Can you show me what "angry" looks like? *Pause and let the children show angry faces.* That looks pretty scary. Elijah wasn't afraid of the king because he knew that he was doing the right thing by worshipping only God. Elijah told the king to have everyone get together at Mount Carmel so that they all could learn who they were really supposed to worship and love.

In the morning, when everyone was gathered together, Elijah said to the people, "You can't have it both ways! If Baal is god, then worship Baal; but if the Lord is God, then worship the Lord." The people didn't say anything. Then Elijah said,

"We will set up everything for two fires, but we won't light them." What do you think the people used to set up the fires? *Pause and let the children share their ideas of what would be needed for a fire*. Let's pretend we are setting up fires. *Pause and help the children gather up the twigs and set up two fires*. Elijah told everyone, "You call on the gods you worship to light your fire, and then I will call on the Lord to light my fire. The god who answers by lighting the fire is the one you should worship." What do you think will happen? *Pause and let the children respond*. Let's find out what happened that day. The 450 followers of Baal began to shout and march around, calling to Baal to light their fire. They shouted and marched from early morning until noon, and nothing happened! What else could they possibly do to get an answer? *Pause and let the children share ideas of how they could get an answer from someone who didn't answer*. Elijah told them maybe it would help if they shouted louder or danced more. "Maybe," Elijah said, "your god is somewhere else and can't hear you." Can you show me how they might have danced around and shouted to get their god's attention? *Have the children dance around, shouting; encourage them (as Elijah did) to shout louder and dance harder. Have the congregation help with the shouting so that it gets really loud*. You did a great job, but what do you think happened that day? *Pause and let the children share their ideas of what happened*. The 450 people shouted and danced around on and on until late in the afternoon, but there was still no answer, no voice, no fire!

Then Elijah told all of the people to come over by him while he set up his fire. After he had everything in place, he told the people to pour water on the wood. Do you think a fire would light if the wood were wet? *Pause and let the children respond*. Elijah told the people to pour water on the wood three times so it would be really soaked. Then Elijah said, "O Lord, God of Abraham, Isaac and Israel, let it be known today that you are God in Israel and that I am your servant and have done all these things at your command. Answer me, O Lord, answer me, so these people will know that you, O Lord, are God, and that you are turning their hearts back again." What do you think happened then? *Pause and let the children respond*. After Elijah prayed to the Lord, the fire of the Lord came and burned up everything that Elijah had set up for his fire and even dried up all of the water that was standing around the fire. When the people saw this, they began saying, "The Lord—he is God! The Lord—he is God!" Let's say that together. *Pause for children to respond*. Wow! God really came through, didn't he? God and Elijah showed the people in a very powerful way who they should worship and serve.

Open your Bible to Exodus 20:2-3, and show the page to the children. In the Bible, God says, **"I am the Lord your God, who brought you out of Egypt, out of the land of slavery. You shall have no other gods before me."** This is the first of the Ten Commandments, and it says that we should worship only the one, true God. He should be first place in our lives, just as he was first place in Elijah's life. Can you think of anything that people do today that seems to place God somewhere other than first place? *Pause and let the children respond. If they struggle for answers, you may want to suggest some answers such as money, sports, and possessions*. We can show others by our actions that God is in first place in our lives. Can you think of ways that we can make God number one?

Pause and let the children share their ideas. For example, they may say things such as telling others about God, helping others, or praying.

Let's pray together and thank God for being in first place in our lives. Dear God, thank you for showing us your power and love. Help us always to remember that you are the one true God, and help us always to worship only you. In Jesus' name, amen.

God Speaks to Elijah in a Whisper

Bible Story: 1 Kings 19:9-18

Bible Verse: "So do not fear, for I am with you; do not be dismayed, for I am your God. I will strengthen you and help you; I will uphold you with my righteous right hand" (Isaiah 41:10).

Simple Supplies: *You'll need a Bible.*

A s children are getting settled, begin to whisper. *Can you hear me? Pause. Can you hear me now? Pause. Now can you hear me? If you can hear me, raise your hand. Pause for children to respond. When it's quiet and children's hands are raised, continue in a soft voice.* You can put your hands down. Thank you for listening so closely that you could hear me when I whispered. I want to tell you about a time when God whispered.

A long time ago there was a man named Elijah. He was a good man, and he was faithful to God. He tried very hard to tell the people to obey God, but they wouldn't listen. In fact, the people were tired of hearing Elijah talk about God, and they wanted to kill him! Elijah felt very alone, and he was worried. He was afraid for his life! Elijah went to a mountain to talk with God about what to do.

When Elijah got to the mountain, great and mighty winds began to blow. *Can you make the sound of the wind? Pause to allow children to respond.* Elijah listened for the voice of God in the wind, but God wasn't in the wind.

Then there was an earthquake! The ground shook, and Elijah trembled. *Can you shake your body like you're in an earthquake? Pause to allow children to respond.* Elijah listened for the voice of God in the earthquake, but God wasn't in the earthquake.

Then Elijah saw a fire. It had flames that reached to the sky. *Can you reach to the sky like the fire did? Pause to allow children to respond.* Elijah listened for the voice of God in the fire, but God wasn't in the fire.

Then Elijah heard a whisper. Elijah stood very still. He knew it was the voice of God. Elijah listened very carefully. God told Elijah not to worry and not to be afraid. God promised Elijah that he would take care of him. *Can you whisper to* your neighbor? Let's whisper, "I'll help you." *Allow time for the children to whisper to one another.*

God wants us to listen for his voice. He wants to help us. God wants to make us strong in him. If you were tempted to do something wrong and you bowed your head and prayed, God would help you know what to do. God will help us to be strong when we are tempted to do wrong things. Can you think of other times that you might need to listen for God's voice? *Pause for children to respond.*

I want to teach you a little rhyme: "I will listen when I pray; I know God's voice will lead the way." *Show the children how to cup their hands around their ears when they say "listen" and point straight in front of themselves for the words "lead the way."* Say the rhyme with me and use the hand motions. "I will listen when I pray; I know God's voice will lead the way." I'd like you to remember this rhyme and say it, either out loud or to yourself, the next time you feel like you need to hear God's voice.

Open your Bible to Isaiah 41:10, and show the page to the children. Isaiah 41:10 says, **"So do not fear, for I am with you; do not be dismayed, for I am your God. I will strengthen you and help you; I will uphold you with my right-eous right hand."** God promises that he will strengthen and help us. And we must remember that we don't always have to look for God in big things. God is in the mighty wind, but God is also in a little flower. God is always near. God was near to Elijah, so near that he could whisper. God whispered to Elijah that he would take care of him. Elijah heard God's voice, and he knew that God would lead the way. *Lead children in prayer.*

Dear God, thank you for taking care of Elijah. Thank you that you promise to always help us, too. Thank you that we are never alone because you are always near, near enough to whisper. In Jesus' name, amen.

God Takes Elijah to Heaven

Bible Story: 2 Kings 2:1-15

> **Bible Verse: "So whether you eat or drink or whatever you do, do it all for the glory of God" (1 Corinthians 10:31).**

Simple Supplies: *You'll need a Bible, an empty paper-towel tube, red construction paper, and tape.*

Israel was in trouble. Bad Israelite kings followed fake gods. Selfish queens planned murder. Israel had suffered three years without rain. Even war had left the country in ruins. However, God was not about to give up on his beloved Israel. He sent the prophet Elijah to warn the Israelites and to encourage them to follow the Lord.

Elijah had been a powerful teacher, a force kings and commanders feared, a healing river, and one of Israel's greatest prophets. Nothing and no one could stop him from following all of God's commands and speaking all of God's words. Whatever he did, he did it for God. An amazing end was about to come to this amazing man. It was time for Elijah to pass on the torch to his friend and student, Elisha.

Have you ever seen or been in a re- lay race? In a relay race, one team member runs around the track and then hands the baton *(hold up the paper-towel tube)* to the next team member. That person runs around the track and then passes the baton on to the next team member. Then that person runs and finally passes the baton on to the last team member. If that person crosses the finish line before the other peo- ple, the whole team wins. *Give the baton to one child.*

Elijah was ready to pass on the baton to Elisha. As I tell this story, after every few lines I'd like you to pass the baton to the person sitting next to you. We're all on the same team, and we're trying to win in our race for the Lord.

When the Lord was about to take Elijah up to heaven, his friend and student, Elisha, went with him. Elijah said to Elisha, "Stay here; the Lord has sent me to Bethel." Pass the baton to the next person.

But Elisha said, "As surely as the Lord lives...I will not leave you." So Elisha went with Elijah to Bethel. There many prophets came out to Elisha and said, "Do you know that the Lord is going to take your master from you today?"

How did they know? That's right. Prophets are given words of wisdom from God. Pass the baton to the next person.

"Yes, I know," Elisha replied, "but do not speak of it." It made Elisha too sad to think that after today he would no longer see his teacher and friend, Elijah. Pass the baton to the next person.

When they went to Jericho, more prophets came out and stood a little ways away. Pass the baton to the next person.

At the river Jordan, Elijah took his cloak, rolled it up and struck the water with it. Miraculously, the water divided to the right and the left, and the two of them crossed over on dry ground. Squish, squash, through soggy sand they walked. The fifty prophets watched with their mouths hanging opened in astonishment as they crossed from the shore.

It was time. Elijah turned to his friend and asked, "Before I leave, what can I do for you?"

Did Elisha ask to be famous or powerful? No. Elisha asked for even more of Elijah's spirit so he could continue to be God's prophet.

Elijah said, "Hmm, you've asked for a huge thing. If God decides to give you my power, you'll know it because you will see me taken away."

Suddenly, a blazing chariot of fire and horses swept from out of the sky. The winds whirled around the chariot. Elisha looked up as the chariot disappeared into the sky, taking Elijah home to heaven.

Elisha shouted above the whirling winds, "My father! My father! The chariots and horsemen of Israel!" He was crying out that the help of Israel was now gone.

And Elisha saw him no more. Elisha was so overwhelmed by sadness, loneliness, and emptiness that he took his clothes and tore them apart. "What will I do," he must have thought. After he lay on the ground weeping, he got up to drag himself back home. What was that piece of cloth? He picked it up. It was Elijah's cloak, and it hadn't been burned up. It was God's baton. The help of Israel was now given to Elisha.

Elisha picked up that robe. He struck the river Jordan with the little strength he had left. When he struck it, the waters divided. Elisha ran through that opened river. He knew. He knew God was with him and always would be.

Elisha went on to be God's prophet and did the work Elijah had begun, the work God had given him to do. *Open your Bible to 1 Corinthians 10, and show the page to the children.* 1 Corinthians 10:31 says, **"So whether you eat or drink or whatever you do, do it all for the glory of God."**

Elisha knew that God was with him always, and he wanted to do everything he did for God's glory. What do you think it means to do everything for God's glory? *Pause for children's responses.* How can you do things, even the things you don't like to do very much, for God's glory? *Pause for children's responses.* When we try to do everything in our lives for God's glory, he can do great things through us, just as he did great things through Elijah and Elisha. *Give each child a piece of red construction paper.* I'd like you to roll your construction paper into a baton just like the one you were passing around earlier. *Give children tape to hold their batons together.* I'd like you to take these batons home. When you look at them, they can remind you that we can do everything in our lives for the glory of God.

Let's pray together. Dear God, just as Elijah passed on a fiery faith to Elisha, I would like to pass on a fiery faith to these children. Whatever they do, may they do it for you. In Jesus' name, amen.

Jehoshaphat Trusts God for Victory

Bible Story: 2 Chronicles 20:1-30

> **Bible Verse:** "Cast all your anxiety on him because he cares for you" (1 Peter 5:7).

Simple Supplies: *You'll need a Bible, resealable plastic bags, confetti, and a handheld vacuum cleaner. Put a small amount of confetti in each plastic bag. You'll need one bag for each child.*

Raise your hand if you play a sport such as soccer, baseball, or basketball. *Pause.* Raise your hand if you take ballet, gymnastics, or piano lessons. *Pause.* Do any of you feel nervous right before you hit a ball or perform in a show? *Pause for children to respond.* When are some other times that you've felt nervous or even afraid? *Pause for children to respond.* Well, I want to tell you about a man named Jehoshaphat who was very afraid. Can you show me a scared face? *Pause for children to respond.* That's exactly how Jehoshaphat looked. Whenever I say the word "afraid," I'd like you to make a scared face. Jehoshaphat was the king of Judah, and he had to lead his people into battle against some very strong enemies. Show me your muscles. *Pause for children to respond.* Whenever I say the word "strong," I need for you to show me your muscles. The strong armies *(pause for children to show their muscles)* of the enemies had a whole lot more men than the army of King Jehoshaphat, and he was really afraid. *Pause for children to make scared faces.* What are some things that you can do to help you not be afraid? *Pause for children to respond.* A great thing to do when you're afraid is to pray. *Pause for children to make scared faces.* You can tell God that you're scared and ask him to help you to be brave. That's exactly what Jehoshaphat did. He asked all of the people throughout Judah, every man, woman, and child, to pray. They all prayed to God to help them during the battle against their strong enemies. *Pause for children to show their muscles.* Guess what happened when Jehoshaphat's army went to battle? *Pause.* They were victorious. What does victorious mean? *Pause for children to respond.* Victorious means that they won! Let's all shout, "Hip, hip, hooray!" *Repeat again and have children shout it with you.* God helped Jehoshaphat's army defeat the enemies.

Open your Bible to 1 Peter 5:7, and show the page to the children.

First Peter 5:7 says, **"Cast all your anxiety on him because he cares for you."** That means that whenever we are worried or afraid about something, we can give it to God. *Pause for children to make scared faces.* One way that we can do that is through prayer. We can ask God to help us not to be worried or afraid. *Pause for children to make scared faces.* Jehoshaphat was very afraid, but he knew that he could trust God to help him. Jehoshaphat prayed and asked God to help him defeat his enemies. Just as Jehoshaphat did, we can turn over all of our worries to God. What are some things that worry you? *Allow children time to share some of their worries.*

Give each child a plastic bag filled with confetti. Let's pretend that this bag is filled with things that you're worried about or things that scare you like *(mention some of the worries that the children just mentioned).*

Remember the verse we just read? **"Cast all your anxiety on him because he cares for you."** On the count of three, I want you to reach in your bag and grab a handful of "worries" and throw them up to God. Ready? One, two, three! *Pause for children to throw their confetti into the air.* Next time that you're worried or afraid (*pause for children to make scared faces),* what can you do? *Pause for children to respond.* You can pray and give your worries to God.

Let's thank God for taking away our worries.
Dear God, thank you for loving us and helping us. When we are afraid or lonely or worried, we can ask you to take those feelings away and we know that you will. Help us to be like Jehoshaphat and come to you when we need you. In Jesus' name, amen.

Take a moment to clean up the confetti while children are returning to their seats.

SECTION

TWO

WINTER
QUARTER

Get Ready for Jesus

Bible Story: Isaiah 2:1-5

> **Bible Verse:** "For God did not send his Son into the world to condemn the world, but to save the world through him" (John 3:17).

Simple Supplies: *You'll need a Bible, a small undecorated Christmas tree, some plastic ornaments, a string of garland, a treetop star, jingle bells, string or yarn, and scissors. String each jingle bell onto a length of string or yarn; you'll need one jingle-bell necklace for each child.*

Place the Christmas tree on the floor in front of the children. Point to the tree. Who can tell me what this is? *Pause for children to respond.* This is a Christmas tree, but it seems to be missing some things. Does it look like it's ready for Christmas? *Pause for children to respond.* This tree isn't ready for Christmas, is it? *Pause.* What do we need to do to get this tree ready for Christmas? *Pause for children to respond.* I just happen to have some things that we can use to

FIND EGGS

get this tree ready for Christmas. *Hand the garland to two children and let them wrap it around the tree. Then give ornaments to several children to hang on the tree. Hold the star in front of you before the children.* What are we missing? *Pause.* Yes, we need to place the star on top. *Give the star to a child and allow him or her to place the star on top of the tree.* Our tree looks so much better. Now it's ready for Christmas.

Decorating trees is one way that we can get ready for Christmas. What are some other ways that you get ready for Christmas? *Pause for children to respond.* Why do we celebrate Christmas? *Pause.* We celebrate Christmas because it is the birthday of Jesus, God's greatest gift to us. In the Bible, a man named Isaiah told the people to get ready for the coming of Jesus too. He told them about the wonderful things that Jesus would bring. What did Jesus do when he was here on earth? *Pause for children to respond.* Isaiah told the people that Jesus would teach them about God. Jesus would show them how to worship and how to pray. Jesus would show them how to love. He would bring hope and peace. Was Isaiah right? *Pause for children to respond.* Jesus is God among us, and we are to try to be just like him. Each year when we celebrate Christmas, we can take some time to prepare our hearts to get ready for Jesus and to try to follow his ways.

Open your Bible to John 3:17, and show the page to the children.

John 3:17 says, **"For God did not send his Son into the world to condemn the world, but to save the world through him."**

That means that God didn't send Jesus to punish us, but to save us. What did Jesus come to save us from? *Pause for children to respond.* God sent Jesus to save us from our sin. Everybody sins, no matter who they are. This verse shows us how much God really loves us. Even though we do bad things, God forgives us and he loves us so much that he sent Jesus to save us from the bad things that we do.

Give each child a jingle-bell necklace. I want you to wear this jingle bell as a reminder to get your heart ready for Jesus. I'd like you to wear it around your ~~neck~~ close to your heart. Every time your bell jingles, ask yourself if you are acting like Jesus. Ask God to help you to be more like him. + if others hear the jingle, tell them about

wrist

Let's thank God for sending Jesus. Dear God, thank you for the greatest gift there is...Jesus. Help us to get our hearts ready for him and to walk in your way. Thank you for sending Jesus to save the world. In Jesus' name, amen.

the great news of Jesus.

Solomon Tells of Jesus' Coming

Bible Story: Psalm 72:1-19

Bible Verse: "For there is one God and one mediator between God and men, the man Christ Jesus" (1 Timothy 2:5).

Simple Supplies: *You'll need a Bible and award ribbons.*

A s the children come forward, begin to look for award-worthy characteristics, and give each child one award ribbon. For example, you might ask, "Who is kind? Billy, are you kind? That's a great thing. I have an award ribbon for a boy who is kind." Be sure to say, "That's a great thing" with the distribution of each ribbon.

You all have award ribbons! I am so proud of all of you. *Take a few moments to list all of the things you gave ribbons for.* Can anyone think of some other great things? *Pause for children's responses.* Those are great things too. Doing great things makes God happy.

A man named Solomon lived many years ago. He knew that God was going to send Jesus to earth to do great things. Solomon was excited, and he told everyone that Jesus was coming. Solomon told the people that Jesus would come to do great things. A moment ago I gave each of you a ribbon for doing something important, and I said, "That's a great thing." As I tell you about the great things Solomon said Jesus would do, can you say, "That's a great thing" after each one?

Let's practice once. *Pause to lead the children in saying, "That's a great thing."*

Solomon told the people that Jesus would teach us about right and wrong, and that he would be fair. *Pause for the children to say, "That's a great thing."* Yes, that is a great thing. And Solomon said that Jesus would help people who were hurting. *Pause for children to chant, "That's a great thing."* Solomon knew more. He told the people that Jesus would come to love kids who are in need. *Pause for children to say, "That's a great thing."* Solomon also explained that Jesus would always be alive and that he would be the way for us to go to God. *Pause for the children to say, "That's a great thing."*

We have named some of the great things that Solomon said that Jesus would do. Jesus does great things in my life every day. Can you name some great things that Jesus has done for you? *Allow the children to respond. After each answer, say, "Yes, [child's name], that's a great thing that Jesus has done for you."*

I am so glad to hear all the great things Jesus has done for all of you. Isn't it wonderful that Jesus does great things in our lives? Solomon was excited and he told everyone about Jesus. We should be excited too. We should tell people about all of the great things Jesus does.

Open your Bible to 1 Timothy 2:5, and show the page to the children.

First Timothy 2:5 says, **"For there is one God and one mediator between God and men, the man Christ Jesus."** Solomon let everyone know that Jesus would do great things. Jesus was born, just as the Scriptures said he would be. And Jesus did great things when he lived on earth. But it didn't stop there! Jesus is still doing great things today. Many of you shared the great things Jesus is doing in your lives.

One of the greatest things that Jesus does is to make a way for us to go to God. If I lift you up and carry you to your family, then I would make a way for you to go to your family. That's almost like what Jesus does. He carries us in his arms to God. And that's a really great thing.

Let's pray together. Dear God, thank you for sending Jesus to do great things. Thank you that because of Jesus, we can come to you. In Jesus' name, amen.

Don't forget to take your award ribbons with you. When you look at your ribbon, remember the great things that Jesus does.

An Angel Appears to Joseph

Bible Story: Matthew 1:18-25

Bible Verse: " 'For I know the plans I have for you,' declares the Lord, 'plans to prosper you and not to harm you, plans to give you hope and a future' " (Jeremiah 29:11).

Simple Supplies: *You'll need a Bible and a set of building blocks.*

Do you like to build things? *Pause for children to respond.* A man named Joseph in the Bible was a carpenter. He built wagons, chairs, and tables using a hammer, nails, and a saw. It's wonderful to create, isn't it? Let's build something along with Joseph. While Joseph zipped and pound-pound-pounded in the woodshop, he was also building a dream. *Hand each child a block. Use one block to create the foundation for a tower. As you share the following story, have one child add his or her block to the tower after each sentence. Open your Bible to Matthew 1:18-25, and show the children the page.*

Joseph daydreamed about his bride-to-be, Mary. *Add a block.*

He said to himself, "I have a plan. Someday I plan to marry her." *Add a block.*

Then I plan that later we will have children. *Add a block.*

Then I'll plan to build a house for us. *Add a block.*

Much later, my home will be full of giggles and laughter. *Add a block.*

Mary will bake my favorite bread. *Add a block.*

I'll hug her every night. *Add a block.*

I'll tell stories to all my children. *Add a block.*

Joseph would put down his measuring line and give a happy sigh. *Add a block.*

Oh, Joseph had plans. *Add a block.*

Until one day, when Mary came to see him. With two little words, all of Joseph's sweet plans came tumbling down around him. Mary said, "Joseph, I'm pregnant." *Push the tower over and leave the blocks lying there.*

Joseph wanted to scream, "No, no, no! This is not the plan. We aren't married yet! That wasn't supposed to happen yet! God, what are you doing? Why is this happening? I thought you had plans to give me hope and a future!" Joseph was so confused. Alone in the darkness of the night, he tossed and turned, wondering what he should do. He must have felt like a leaf blowing in the wind, or like a piece of this broken tower. "Why, God, why? I'm scared. I'm sad. I'm confused..." Finally, Joseph drifted off to sleep. *Pause.*

In the middle of the night, Joseph felt a touch upon his shoulder. He opened his eyes, but the room was so bright, he shut them instantly. "Joseph, son of David," a firm, yet soft voice said. Joseph's eyes snapped open. His jaw dropped but no sound came out. As Joseph's eyes adjusted to the light, he saw a being so gentle and powerful that he knew it was an angel of the Lord. The angel said, "Joseph, son of David, do not be afraid to take Mary home as your wife. The child growing inside her is the Son of God's Holy Spirit. This is not an ordinary child. Mary will give birth to a son, and you are to name him Jesus, because he will save his people from their sins."

Joseph tried to leap to his feet but he couldn't. He remembered a passage from Scripture. Hundreds of years ago, Isaiah had foretold that this day would come. It was written in the Old Testament of the Bible: "The virgin will be with child and will give birth to a son, and will call him Immanuel" (Isaiah 7:14). Immanuel—that means "God with us."

Joseph mumbled over and over, "God with us, God with us, God with us." Then he sat up. In the morning light, he said it aloud, "God with us. Wow!" The angel was gone. Joseph jumped up. He shook his head and ran to Mary's house. He picked her up and hugged her carefully.

"Mary, Mary, God sent an angel to me last night. I thought I had a plan, but God had a better plan. Come on," he said. "We're going to get married. And then we're going home."

Mary went home with Joseph. She did give birth to God's Son. And Joseph gave him the name Jesus. That is how the birth of Jesus Christ came about.

Sometimes we think our plans are the best. But God's plans are better. I'd like each of you to take a block. While I say this verse, you can shape the blocks into the best Christmas gift God ever gave the world, the cross of Jesus. For that is why Jesus came, to save his people from their sins. *Help children form a cross with the blocks.*

Open your Bible to Jeremiah 29:11, and show the page to the children. Jeremiah 29:11 says, " 'For I know the plans I have for you,' declares the Lord, 'plans to prosper you and not to harm you, plans to give you hope and a future.' "

Now I'd like each of you to hold a block and pray with me while I talk to God.

Dear God, you know the plans you have for us, and they are for good. Thank you for your wonderful plan of sending Jesus to save us from our sins. Jesus, Immanuel, you are with us. Thank you! In Jesus' name, amen.

Jesus Is Born

Bible Story: Luke 2:1-20; Hebrews 1:1-4

> **Bible Verse: "Jesus answered, 'I am the way and the truth and the life. No one comes to the Father except through me' "** **(John 14:6).**

Simple Supplies: *You'll need a Bible, a baby doll, a roll of white streamers, scissors, a pen or marker, and a towel or blanket. Cut the roll of white streamers into eleven two-foot lengths. Use a pen or marker to write one of these phrases on each strip of streamer: "The Savior," "Christ the Lord," "Heir of all things (the whole earth will be his one day)," "Creator of the universe," "The radiance (the sunshine) of God's glory," "The exact image of God," "He takes away our sin," "He is at the right hand of the majesty in heaven," "More powerful than the angels," "God's Son," and "The way, the truth, and the life." Wrap the baby in the streamers and cover the baby with a baby blanket.*

Why does the whole world take a day to celebrate the birth of one little Jewish boy? Why do we sing songs about him? Why do we build churches and go to them to learn about a baby who was born so far away and long ago? Who is Jesus?

Open your Bible to Luke 2:1-20, and show the page to the children. In those days Caesar Augustus, the emperor, made a law that everyone needed to be counted. So Joseph had to go back to his town of Bethlehem, about seventy miles away. He took Mary with him. Mary was very pregnant, huge and heavy with the baby inside. While they were in Bethlehem, the time came for the baby to be born, and Mary gave birth to her firstborn, a son. *Bring out the doll and cradle it.* She wrapped the baby in strips of cloth and placed him in a manger because there was no room for them in the inn.

And there were shepherds in the fields nearby, keeping watch over their flocks at night. An angel of the Lord appeared to them, and the glory of the Lord shone around them, and they were terrified. How would you feel if you saw an angel? *Pause.*

But the angel said, "Do not be afraid. I bring you good news of great joy that will be for all the people. Today in the town of David a Savior has been born to you; he is Christ the Lord. This will be a sign to you: You will find a baby wrapped in cloths and lying in a manger."

Suddenly the entire sky burst with light. The silent night was filled with singing, cheering, joyous angels shouting the good news, spilling this great news out, "Glory to God in the highest!" And this astounding favor, this gift, this love is also for you. The God of the highest heavens has come down to earth to make peace—to choose to be a friend to you. What greater news could there be?

So the shepherds hurried off and found this baby. And what did they find? Did they find an infant who wore a golden crown who could speak ten languages and wore a diamond-studded purple robe? No. They found a baby who looked like any other baby, wrapped in strips of cloth because no one had even given Mary baby clothes. So what child is this? Who is this baby that angels greet, kings lay at his feet, and a brilliant star came to meet? Let's unwrap the truth.

Let twelve children each unwrap one of the "strips of cloth" from the baby doll. Help each child read his or her strip aloud. These words and phrases tell us why Jesus came; he came to help us. Because of Jesus, we can get close to God and learn to be more like him. What an amazing gift God gave us at Christmas!

When the shepherds had seen Jesus, they told everyone about him! All who heard the news were amazed at what the shepherds said to them. All the shepherds did was tell the truth about what they saw, heard, and knew. And we can tell the truth about Jesus too. Who is Jesus Christ?

Open your Bible to John 14:6, and show the page to the children. John 14:6 says, **"Jesus answered, 'I am the way and the truth and the life. No one comes to the Father except through me.' "** This verse reminds us that Jesus came to point the way to God and to help us know God. Can you say the verse with me? *Repeat the verse with the children.*

Let's pray together. Dear Jesus, you created the universe. You are the radiance of God's glory. You are far above the angels. And you didn't forget us. You came to us. You made a way for us to make peace with you. Jesus, you are the way, the truth, and the life. Glory to you in the highest! In Jesus' name, amen.

foreign Visitors Worship Jesus

Bible Story: Matthew 2:1-12

> **Bible Verse:** "For there is no difference between Jew and Gentile—the same Lord is Lord of all and richly blesses all who call on him, for 'Everyone who calls on the name of the Lord will be saved' " (Romans 10:12-13).

Simple Supplies: *You'll need a Bible and star stickers. Cut the stickers so that each child will have one, and keep the paper backing on the stickers. Hide the stickers around the area. Practice the following poem several times before sharing it with the children. Speed up the pace of the poem as it progresses and as you become comfortable with the rhythm.*

The Bible says that everyone who calls upon the name of the Lord will be saved. If you are looking for Jesus, you'll find him. We're going to share our Bible story today in the form of a poem. *Open your Bible to Matthew 2:1-12, and show the children the words.* I'd like for you to act out the motions with me.

This is Jesus. *(Hold your arms as if cradling a baby.)*

This is Jesus, in Mary's arms. *(Rock your arms in a cradle motion.)*

Who would do a baby harm? *(Hold your palms up and shrug your shoulders.)*

Joy is finding Jesus.

These are the wise men who came from afar. *(Hold your hand over your eyes as if looking far away.)*

They traveled the hills and followed the star *(Point up.)*

To find Jesus in Mary's arms. *(Rock your arms in a cradle motion.)*

Who would do a baby harm? *(Hold your palms up and shrug your shoulders.)*

Joy is finding Jesus.

This is Jerusalem. King Herod lives there. *(Hold your hands up to your head to form a "crown.")*

The wise men asked him, "Where, oh where *(Scratch your head and look puzzled.)*

Is the baby, born to be king? *(Hold your arms out.)*

The one of whom the angels sing?"

Asked the wise men who came from afar, *(Hold your hand over your eyes as if looking far away.)*

Who traveled the hills and followed the star, *(Point up.)*

The star that leads to Mary's arms,

(Rock your arms in a cradle motion.)

Protecting Jesus from all harm.

Joy is finding Jesus.

This is King Herod, getting mad, *(Put on a mad face.)*

But smart enough to pretend he's glad. *(Run your hand over your face and turn your mad face into a glad face.)*

He gathered the priests into a committee. *(Make a "come here" motion with your index finger.)*

Herod asked them, "Into which city

Is this king to be born and live?" *(Scratch your head and look puzzled.)*

He lied about the worship he'd give *(Bow your head.)*

To the baby born to be king, *(Hold your arms out.)*

The one of whom the angels sing.

He lied to the wise men who came from afar, *(Hold your hand over your eyes as if looking far away.)*

Who traveled the hills to follow the star, *(Point up.)*

To find Jesus in Mary's arms. *(Rock your arms in a cradle motion.)*

Who would do a baby harm? *(Hold your palms up and shrug your shoulders.)*

Joy is finding Jesus.

This is Bethlehem, the little town *(Hold your hands out, palms up.)*

To whom the Savior of earth came down.

Bethlehem, said the prophets of old

Is the town we've long been told

Where the babe would be born— the tiny king, *(Hold your hands up to your head to form a "crown.")*

The one of whom the angels sing.

The wise men went there, who came from afar. *(Hold your hand over your eyes as if looking far away.)*

They traveled the hills to follow the star, *(Point up.)*

To find Jesus in Mary's arms. *(Rock your arms in a cradle motion.)*

Who would do a baby harm? *(Hold your palms up and shrug your shoulders.)*

Joy is finding Jesus.

This is the smile upon the face *(Smile.)*

Of everyone in every place.

Look at the light, the star of joy, *(Point up.)*

The happiness at finding the boy!

These are the gifts: "We worship— behold *(Kneel on one knee.)*

Take our frankincense, myrrh, and gold."

They gave their gifts and worshipped the king, *(Hold your arms out in front.)*

The one of whom the angels sing.

The wise men bowed who came from afar. *(Hold your hand over your eyes as if looking far away.)*

They traveled the hills to follow the star. *(Point up.)*

They found Jesus in Mary's arms. *(Rock your arms in a cradle motion.)*

Who would do a baby harm? *(Hold your palms up and shrug your shoulders.)*

Joy is finding Jesus.

Have you found your joy in Jesus?

Good job! Thank you for helping me tell the Bible story! The wise men searched long and hard for the baby they had heard would be king. I've hidden some things in this room that can remind us of the wise men's search for Jesus. Let's see if you can find them; there's one for each of you. *Help children find the stickers. Have children put the stickers near their hearts.* The wise men followed a star to find Jesus, and then they worshipped him with their whole hearts. Even though they came from another country, the wise men were welcome to come and worship Jesus, the baby

king. Everyone can worship Jesus, because Jesus came for everyone. Romans 10:12-13 says, **"For there is no difference between Jew and Gentile—the same Lord is Lord of all and richly blesses all who call on him, for 'Everyone who calls on the name of the Lord will be saved.' "**

This verse tells us that Jesus will richly bless all who call on him. What do you think that means? *Pause for children's responses.* That's right—if we look for Jesus and turn to him in sincere worship, he will bring good things into our lives. And any one of us can worship Jesus, because Jesus came to save everyone, no matter the color of our skin or the language that we speak. The wise men brought special gifts to Jesus as a form of worship. What are some ways you can show Jesus your worship? *Pause for children's responses.* Good—you can come to church and Sunday school to hear about the wonderful things Jesus has done, you can sing songs and pray prayers thanking Jesus for coming to earth, and you can tell other people about your wonderful Savior.

Let's pray together and thank Jesus for the joy we find in him. Dear Jesus, you are our happiness. Joy is finding you. Please help us each to come to you in worship. Thank you. In Jesus' name, amen.

Joseph Takes His Family to Safety in Egypt
Bible Story: Matthew 2:13-23

> **Bible Verse:** "The Lord is good, a refuge in times of trouble. He cares for those who trust in him" (Nahum 1:7).

Simple Supplies: *You'll need a Bible, a quilt or blanket large enough to fit over several children's laps, a few sheets of newsprint, and small square swatches of blanket fabric such as flannel or fleece, one for each child.*

Hold up the blanket or quilt. Do you see what I'm holding? *Give children time to answer.* Yes! I am holding a nice, warm, cozy quilt. And what is this? *Hold up newsprint and pause for response.* This is newsprint. It's the paper that newspapers are printed on. I'm going to use these two things to help me explain God's love for each of us.

If you were alone in your bedroom at night and feeling just a little afraid of the dark, which one of these might help you to feel safe? *Pause for responses. Spread the quilt over several children's legs, and tuck in the edges to give them the feeling of coziness.* Yes! I agree! I know that I would want to get way down in my bed and cover up with my blanket. *Now "tuck" in another group of children with a few sheets of newsprint.* How does that feel? Warm? Safe? *Pause.* No, this doesn't give you a very safe feeling at all, does it?

In our Bible, we can read these words. *Open your Bible to Nahum 1:7 and show the page to the children:* Nahum 1:7 says, **"The Lord is good, a refuge in times of trouble. He cares for those who trust in him."** When we are afraid, or lonely, or really feeling small in this great big world, all we have to do is ask God to be with us and he will be! Would each of you hold hands with the person you're sitting next to? *Pause and wait for children to hold hands.* Now every time I say the word "trust," I'd like you to squeeze your neighbor's hand. Don't squeeze too hard. We don't want to hurt anyone, do we? Let's practice our little hand squeeze. *Say "trust" and have everyone squeeze the hands they are holding.* Good! Our trust *(pause)* in God is the same trust *(pause)* that we have in our parents. When you wake up in the morning, you *know* that someone will be there to help you get dressed and help you with breakfast. That is trust. *Pause.* To trust *(pause)* in God is like knowing that someone will always look after us and protect us.

There are times when we are other places, like at school, where we need to trust. *Pause.* Every morning we walk into our classrooms and trust *(pause)* there will be a teacher there who will greet us and help us with our learning for the day. When you go to school, you trust *(pause)* that teachers and other adults will help you have a safe day.

God is *always* there for us. We can trust *(pause)* him to be there for us when we are with adults and when we are alone. He is there. He will take us, wrap us up in his love, and spread his warmth all through us, just as this very cozy quilt does. I know of a story in the Bible where there are some people who feel safe as if they're wrapped up in a blanket. There are also some people in this story who feel unsafe as if they're wrapped up in newsprint.

Joseph was once very afraid for his family. He needed a safe place for them because King Herod wanted to kill baby Jesus. Herod had been told that Jesus was going to grow up and become the King of Kings! Well, that scared King Herod so much that he ordered all the firstborn children in his kingdom to be killed. This scared Joseph and Mary! But God had a plan, a plan to provide safety for the little family. Joseph had trusted *(pause)* God for such a long time that he knew that God would not let him down now that things looked very scary. Joseph knew that he had God to turn to for help and protection, just as we can turn to our parents or teachers when we need help and protection. Joseph trusted *(pause)* in God when he was scared, and we can trust *(pause)* in God, too, to love and care for us. God told Joseph to take Mary and baby Jesus and go to another country, Egypt, and stay until it was safe to go home. Now which of the two feelings, the blanket or the newsprint, do you think that Joseph and Mary had in Egypt even though they were far from home? *Pause.* Yes, the blanket feeling. That was trust *(pause)* working in a very big way! They knew that they were safe and that God loved them, and so it didn't matter that they were so far away from home.

Inside, King Herod probably felt the warmth of a newspaper. Why? *Children will give a variety of responses. Praise each one.* Yes, it's because he had never known trust *(pause)* in God or God's love for him. Isn't that sad? And aren't we lucky that we do know God and his love and can have the blanket feeling and not the newsprint feeling inside of us? Whew!! That was a lot of hand squeezing, wasn't it? But it's because we should always have a lot of trust in God! I have a little blanket for you to keep as a reminder of God's constant love and the constant trust we can have in Him. *Give each child a swatch of flannel or fleece.*

Let's thank God for his love. Dear God, thank you for loving us and wrapping us in the warm safety of your love when we need it. Help us to remember to tell others about your love and how much they can trust in you. In Jesus' name, amen.

Jesus Is Baptized

Bible Story: Matthew 3:13–17

> **Bible Verse:** "In the beginning was the Word, and the Word was with God, and the Word was God" (John 1:1).

Simple Supplies: *You'll need a Bible; several large pictures of famous people kids will know, such as George Washington, Tiger Woods, Abraham Lincoln, and the pastor; a large picture of Jesus; and a beanbag.*

How many of you have photo albums at your house? *Pause.* Are they filled with pictures of your family and friends? *Pause.* I have some pictures that I want to show to you today. As I show you a picture, I want you to tell me who it is. *Show all of the pictures and allow the children time to identify each one. Show kids the picture of Jesus last.* Who is Jesus? *Pause for children to respond.* Jesus is the Son of God.

Today we're going to talk about a very special baptism—Jesus' baptism. What does it mean to be baptized? Why are people baptized? *Pause for children's responses.* People are baptized as an outward sign of their decisions to walk with God and to follow him in all they do. One day Jesus went down to the Jordan River where John the Baptist was baptizing people. Jesus walked right up to

John and asked to be baptized. John the Baptist said, "I'm the one who should be baptized by you," but Jesus had John baptize him. When Jesus came up from the water in the Jordan River, the heavens opened, and he saw God's Spirit descending like a dove. A voice from heaven said, "This is my Son, with whom I am well-pleased."

Whose voice was that? *Pause.* Yes, it was the voice of God, and he was happy with his Son. Who is Jesus? *Pause.* Yes, Jesus is the Son of God. Let's play a little game to help us remember that Jesus is God's Son. *Hold up the beanbag.* When I throw this beanbag to you, I'll say, "Whose child are you?" and you'll say "I'm [parent's name]'s son [or daughter]." Then I'll say, "Who's Jesus?" and you'll say, "The Son of God." *Do this several times with the children.* Being someone's son or daughter is very important, isn't it? It shows who we belong to. In addition to being our parents' sons and daughters, we are all children of God. Jesus is God's Son. God sent his Son to show us what God is like.

Open your Bible to John 1:1, and show the page to the children.

John 1:1 says, **"In the beginning was the Word, and the Word was with God, and the Word was God."** That means that Jesus was with God in the beginning, Jesus is God made into a person, and Jesus is the Son of God.

Let's thank God for his Son, Jesus. Dear God, thank you for your Son, Jesus. We know that you sent Jesus to save the world. Help us to show Jesus' love to everyone. In Jesus' name, amen.

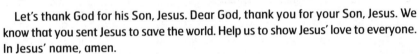

Peter and Andrew Meet Jesus

Bible Story: John 1:35-42

> **Bible Verse:** "Yet to all who received him, to those who believed in his name, he gave the right to become children of God" (John 1:12).

Simple Supplies: *You'll need a Bible, self-adhesive "My name is" tags, and a marker. Use the marker to write "Child of God" after "My name is" on each name tag.*

*A*s the children come forward, hand each child a name tag. Instruct children to peel off the adhesive backing and stick the tags on their clothing. Hi, kids! I've got a little finger play for us to do. You can follow along and do as I do. Hold up your left index finger. This is Papa Bear. Papa Bear is one of the Big Bears of the forest. Papa Bears growl fiercely and loudly. Can you growl fiercely and loudly? Pause to allow children to growl. Then hold up the pinkie finger on your right hand. This is Child Bear. Child Bears growl, too, only not as loud as Papa Bears. Can you growl softly? Pause for children to growl softly.

Child Bear wants to grow up to be just like Papa Bear. Child Bear wants to become one of the Big Bears of the forest. He wants to follow Papa Bear everywhere that he goes so that he can copy everything that Papa Bear does. *Wiggle your right pinkie finger and let it "follow" the left index finger as you move them both in a circle in front of your body.* Can you make your Child Bear follow your Papa Bear? *Pause to give the children time to do the finger play.* That's great. You did a very good job with that. And I think we learned something. If Child Bear follows Papa Bear, he will indeed become one of the Big Bears of the forest.

I know a story from the Bible that is a little like the finger play of Papa Bear and Child Bear. *Hold up your left index finger.* This is Jesus. Jesus was walking one day, and he saw that two men were following him. Their names were James and Andrew. *Hold up the index finger and the second finger of your right hand. Let the right-hand fingers "follow" the left-hand finger.* Can you do this with me? Let's show James and Andrew following Jesus. *Pause for the finger play.*

Jesus asked James and Andrew what they wanted. They said they wanted to follow him. James and Andrew wanted to be with Jesus. They wanted to get to know him. They wanted to learn everything that Jesus could teach them. James and Andrew wanted to be just like Jesus.

Open your Bible to John 1:12, and show the page to the children. John 1:12 says, **"Yet to all who received him, to those who believed in his name, he gave the right to become children of God."** God wants us to follow Jesus. We need to learn all about Jesus. We want to get to know him. Then we can be just like Jesus. Look at the name tag that you are wearing. It says, "My name is Child of God." Because Jesus came to earth and showed us the way to God, we can be called the children of God.

Hold up your left index finger. This is Jesus. *Hold up your right pinkie finger.* This is you. *Wiggle your little finger and let it follow the index finger as you move them both in a circle in front of your body.* Can you make your little finger follow your Jesus finger? *Pause for children to do the finger play.* Once again, you've done a really great job.

We can follow Jesus in our lives every day. We can be with Jesus. We can learn everything that we can about Jesus. We can get to know him. Can you think of some ways that we can learn about Jesus and get to know him? *Pause for children's answers.* That's right. We can listen in church. We can sing praises to Jesus. We can learn what is in the Bible. We can pray and listen closely for Jesus to answer. And just like James and Andrew, we can follow Jesus. It's wonderful to follow Jesus. It's wonderful to be the children of God.

Dear God, thank you for giving us Jesus. Thank you that we can follow Jesus, and that we can get to know him. Help us become like Jesus. Thank you that because of Jesus, we can become your children. In Jesus' name, amen.

Wear your name tag all day today and think about ways you can follow Jesus and get to know him.

News About Jesus Spreads

Bible Story: Matthew 4:23-25

> **Bible Verse:** "Come to me, all you who are weary and burdened, and I will give you rest" (Matthew 11:28).

Simple Supplies: *You'll need a Bible and two cell phones. You'll also need a copy of the Bible story paraphrase (p. 47) for each person in the congregation. Give a helper one of the cell phones and ask him or her to call your cell phone when the children are seated. If you don't have access to cell phones, a simple toy phone that will make a ringing sound can be used.*

Hello? I can't talk right now. I'm trying to give the children's message. Oh, this good news can't wait? Hmm, I see. Wow! That is great news. I'm so glad you're feeling better. You're right. Good news like that just has to be shared. Thanks for calling. *Hang up the phone.*

Hey, kids! It's true—good news has to be shared. What's the best news there ever was? *Pause.* It's not "what," but "who"! Jesus is the best news. He's our healer and our Savior. Listen to what the Bible has to say about Jesus. *Open your Bible to Matthew 4:23-25, and show the children the page.*

Jesus went throughout Galilee, teaching in the synagogues. Synagogues were like the churches we have today. Jesus preached the good news of the kingdom, just as I'm doing now. Jesus healed diseases and sickness among the people. Jesus never went to school to learn how to become a doctor, but he could fix any hurt or illness anyone had. Isn't that amazing? Wouldn't it be wonderful if every person you knew who was sad or sick or crippled became well? What would you ask Jesus to fix for you? *Pause.* What would you ask him to fix for someone else? *Pause.*

Jesus said, **"Come to me, all you who are weary and burdened, and I will give you rest."** The people came to Jesus, and they found rest, comfort, and healing in Jesus.

News about Jesus spread all over Syria, and people brought to Jesus friends who were ill with every kind of disease. Curl your fingers into a fist. Think about people with leprosy whose disease sometimes caused their fingers and toes to fall off. Jesus cured them! Shake your fingers out. Close your eyes. Think about people who stumbled about in a dark world of blindness—now they could see! Open your eyes. Even people who were in terrible pain were made better! Jesus said, **"Come to me, all you who are weary and burdened, and I will give you rest."** When Jesus says he'll do it, he does.

Jesus didn't turn the people away. He didn't say, "Get your act together first and then I'll help you." He said, "Come to me...I will give you help."

Huge crowds of people limped, dragged themselves, stumbled and crawled to Jesus. I would have, wouldn't you? He healed them. He loved them. They loved him. The people told their friends who told their families who told their neighbors about this incredible God-man. Great news like this just can't be kept a secret.

Now let's spread this good news about Jesus. Let's pass around our Bible story to everyone here. *Hand each child a stack of papers and ask them to go throughout the congregation and give one to each person. Be sure each child has a copy also. Then read aloud this simple paraphrase with the children and congregation members.*

After the story is read aloud by the congregation, gather the children to pray.

Dear Jesus, you went around healing people. You are our healer. You are our Savior. You are our helper. We come to you. We are tired and have our own loads to carry. You promised to give us rest. Thank you! In Jesus' name, amen.

Jesus traveled all around the area, sharing the good news of God's love with anyone who would listen. Some people came to him with terrible diseases and in great pain. He put his hands on them, touched them with the great love and power of God, and they were made well. Other people who came to him were blind. He put his warm, gentle hands on their eyes...and they could see again! Other people came to him with great sadness or anger. Jesus held them close and took their bad feelings away. News about the incredible things Jesus did spread throughout the country, and soon, large crowds of people followed Jesus wherever he went. They wanted to know more of this man, this Son of God, who made so many things better.

(Adapted from Matthew 4:23-25)

Jesus Gives the Beatitudes

Bible Story: Matthew 5:1-12

Bible Verse: "Finally, brothers, whatever is true, whatever is noble, whatever is right, whatever is pure, whatever is lovely, whatever is admirable—if anything is excellent or praiseworthy—think about such things" (Philippians 4:8).

Simple Supplies: *You'll need a Bible, paper plates, markers, and glue.*

What is an attitude? *Pause for children's responses.* An attitude is the way we look at something. For example, if your best friend got something you really wanted, how would you feel about that? If you grumbled and complained that your friend got something and you didn't, you would have a bad attitude. If you were happy and excited for your friend, you would have a good attitude. What attitudes do you think make God happy? *Pause for children to answer.*

Today we're going to talk about something that Jesus taught his disciples. He taught them about the attitudes that please God. *Open your Bible to Matthew 5:1-12, and show the page to the children.* Jesus taught that we should always have a happy attitude, knowing that even when things aren't going well or we don't have everything we want, God is blessing us in other ways.

One of the ways God blesses us is by comforting us. Have any of you ever been really sad? I want you to show me your very saddest faces. *Pause for kids to give you their saddest faces.* Whenever we are sad, God wants to comfort us. Now wrap your arms around yourself and give yourself a big hug. Imagine that's what God is doing whenever you are sad.

Another thing God does for us is help us know how to think the right kind of thoughts. That means that when something happens to us that doesn't seem right or fair, we don't get mad, but we wait to see what God will do.

God also shows us mercy. Does anyone know what mercy is? *Pause.* To show mercy means that even when we deserve to be punished for doing something wrong, God is still kind to us. He will always teach us what is right, but sometimes he will be merciful and not give us the punishment we deserve.

Another thing God does for us is to help us see him and know him and be called his children. That's pretty awesome, don't you think?

So, God comforts us, helps us know how to think the right kinds of thoughts, shows us mercy, helps us to see him, and calls us his children. And these are just a few of the many things God does for us!

Finally, God promises a great reward in heaven when people are mean to us because we are Christians. Has anyone ever been mean to you because you are a Christian? What happened? *Allow children to respond.*

Because of all of these things that God does for us, we can have good attitudes. What kinds of things should we think about to have a happy attitude? *Pause.*

Give each child a paper plate and crayons. I want you to draw a picture of a face that shows a happy attitude on one side of your paper plate. Then when you're finished, I want you to draw a picture of a face with a bad attitude on the other side. *Give kids several minutes to draw the faces, making sure that both sides have the face going in the same direction.*

I'm going to name some attitudes people have, and I want you to hold up your faces and show me which kind of attitude you think it is, good or bad. Are you ready?

Name the following attitudes, pausing between them to give children a chance to hold up the faces they've made: angry, sharing, giving, selfish, greedy, thankful, kind, mean, honest.

Let's look at our Bible verse for today to see what God wants us to think about in order to have good attitudes. *Open your Bible to Philippians 4:8, and show the page to the children.* Philippians 4:8 says, **"Finally, brothers, whatever is true, whatever is noble, whatever is right, whatever is pure, whatever is lovely, whatever is admirable—if anything is excellent or praiseworthy—think about such things."**

What do each of these things mean to you? Let's look at what the opposites of these things are. I'll say a word from our verse, and I want you to shout out the word's opposite. *Say the following words, allowing kids to give their responses after each one: true, noble, (you may want to explain that noble means to do the right thing, or to be moral) right, pure, lovely, admirable, excellent, praiseworthy.* All of these words are "happy attitude" words, like your happy face. God wants our minds and hearts to be filled with these good things, even when things in our lives aren't going our way. If we focus on these good things in our hearts and minds, our attitudes and the outward things we do will please God. What are some good things you can think of when things aren't going your way? *Pause for children's responses.*

Let's pray right now and ask God to help us have attitudes that please him. *Lead children in prayer.*

Dear God, help us to always think about the good things you want us to think about and to have attitudes that please you. In Jesus' name, amen.

Jesus Teaches That We Are to Be Salt and Light

Bible Story: Matthew 5:13-16

Bible Verse: "In the same way, let your light shine before men, that they may see your good deeds and praise your Father in heaven" (Matthew 5:16).

Simple Supplies: *You'll need a Bible, a can of soup, a bath towel, a globe, small packets of salt, a flashlight, and a washcloth.*

As the children come forward, hand each child a packet of salt. Save one for yourself and lift it up to look at it. Wow! What do you suppose is in all these little packets? *Pause and allow children to answer.* Yes, all of these packets contain salt. *Hold up the soup can.* Did you know that salt is also in a can of soup? Salt is a preservative. That means it makes the soup last longer. And salt is a seasoning. The salt in the soup makes it tasty and more enjoyable. *Spread the towel and set the globe in the middle. Open a packet of salt and pour it into your hand.* Because salt is made up of tiny little granules, it can really go a long way. *Sprinkle the salt in your hand over the globe.* Jesus said that Christians are supposed to be like salt, spreading the good news of the gospel to all the people of the earth. The good news of Jesus will make people's lives last longer by giving them eternal life in heaven. And just as salt makes food tastier, the good news of Jesus in a life makes it more enjoyable.

Jesus also said that we should be like a light. *Turn on the flashlight.* We should shine Jesus' love in our lives so that all the world can see. *Cover the beam from the flashlight with the washcloth.* What happens to the light when I cover it up? *Pause for children to answer. Then remove washcloth.* Can you put your hands over your eyes? *Pause for children to cover their eyes.* What happens to the light when you cover your eyes? *Pause for answers.* That's right. It gets dark and you can't see the light. *Shine the beam of the flashlight on the globe. Turn the globe gently with your hand so that the light shines on the world.* It is the desire of God's heart that the light of Jesus shine on all the world. *Place the washcloth over the flashlight as you direct it toward the globe.* What happens to the world when the light is covered up? *Pause for the children to answer.* Yes, the world is in darkness. And we don't want the light to be dim. We want Jesus to shine brightly to everyone.

Open your Bible to Matthew 5:16, and show the page to the children. Matthew 5:16 says, **"In the same way, let your light shine before men, that they may see your good deeds and praise your Father in heaven."** God wants the light of Jesus to shine so that all the world can see. God desires his children to be like salt and spread the good news of Jesus to all the people on earth. How can we tell others about Jesus? *Pause for answers.* That's right. We can send food to the needy. We can give money to missionaries. We can love the people in our lives who aren't always so lovable. We can tell others about the wonderful things Jesus has done in our lives.

Let's play a "salt and light" game that helps us remember how we can share Jesus with others. I'll go first. I'm going to share Jesus by inviting my friend to come to church with me. Now, [child's name], come and hold my hand. You tell what you will do. *Continue with the game until everyone who wants to has added a "salt and light" deed and joined hands with those who have already spoken.*

Shine the flashlight under your chin. I can be the light of Jesus. *Flash the light just above children's heads, like a spotlight searching for center stage. Be careful not to shine the light in anyone's eyes.* You can be the light of Jesus too. The world is looking to us to show them Jesus. Let's live in the light.

Dear God, thank you for giving us Jesus. We want everyone to know about Jesus. Help us remember to spread the good news of Jesus like salt and to let the light of Jesus shine in all that we do. In Jesus' name, amen.

Don't forget to take your packet of salt with you. Let the salt remind you to spread the good news of Jesus.

Jesus Walks on Water

Bible Story: Matthew 14:22-33

> **Bible Verse: "If we are faithless, he will remain faithful, for he cannot disown himself" (2 Timothy 2:13).**

Simple Supplies: *You'll need a Bible.*

W e're going on a boat ride today! *Have kids sit and rock back and forth as if they were on a boat. The rocking motion should be slow and gentle.*

Open your Bible to Matthew 14:22-33, and show the page to the kids. In today's Bible story, Jesus' disciples got into a boat and headed for the other side of the lake. *Have kids make a slow rocking motion again.* Jesus wanted to spend some time by himself to pray for a little while.

When Jesus was finished praying, he went to get on the boat with the disciples, but the boat was already far away from the shore. What do you think Jesus did? *Pause for children to answer.* Jesus walked on the water to get to the boat! I want you to stand up and show me what you think it would be like to try to walk on water. *Have kids stand and pretend to walk on water, then sit back down.*

What do you think the disciples thought when they saw Jesus? *Pause.* At first the disciples were afraid because they didn't realize it was Jesus. But Jesus told them who he was and not to be afraid.

What would you have done if you'd seen someone walking on water? One of Jesus' disciples, Peter, wanted Jesus to prove it was really him. So Peter asked Jesus to tell him to come out to him on the water. What do you think happened to Peter? *Pause.* Peter did walk on the water! *Have kids pretend to walk on water again.* But then it got windy and Peter got scared. He began to sink. *Have kids pretend to be scared and sink down into the water.* Then Jesus took hold of Peter and lifted him up. *Have kids reach up their hands as if they were grabbing hold of Jesus' hand and stand back up.*

Jesus asked Peter, "Why did you doubt?" What do you think doubt means? *Pause.* If you doubt, it means you don't really believe something is going to happen. Peter doubted that he could walk on the water as Jesus did, even though he was doing it at the time! Why do you think Peter's doubt caused him to sink into the water? *Pause.* Why do you think Peter became afraid? *Pause.* What do you do when you're afraid? *Pause.* How can not having doubts help you be unafraid? *Pause.*

When Jesus and Peter got back into the boat, the other disciples began to worship Jesus, saying, "Truly you are the Son of God."

Let's look at our Bible verse for today to see what it says about having faith. *Open your Bible to 2 Timothy 2:13, and show the page to the children.* Second Timothy 2:13 says, **"If we are faithless, he will remain faithful, for he cannot disown himself."**

Just as Jesus remained faithful when Peter doubted, Jesus will remain faithful to help us, too. Let's pray right now and ask God to help us have faith even when it's hard to believe. *Lead children in prayer.*

Dear God, thank you that Jesus will always be faithful to be there for us even when we have doubts. Help us to always trust in him. In Jesus' name we pray, amen.

Jesus Explains Eternal Life to Nicodemus

Bible Story: John 3:1-17

Bible Verse: "For God so loved the world that he gave his one and only Son, that whoever believes in him shall not perish but have eternal life" (John 3:16).

Simple Supplies: *You'll need a Bible, dull pennies, plastic tablecloth, salt, water, vinegar, two containers, measuring spoons, a medicine dropper, and moist paper towels. Spread the plastic tablecloth on a low table or on the floor near where children will sit. In one of the containers, make a solution of one teaspoon of salt and one tablespoon of water. Place several tablespoons of vinegar into the other container.*

W e're going to start today's message with an experiment. *Give each child a dull penny.* We're going to do our experiment with these pennies. I want you to set your pennies on this tablecloth. We're going to put something on them to see what happens to them.

Have kids come and place their pennies on the tablecloth. Take the medicine dropper and have a volunteer put a drop of the salt solution on each penny. Then have another volunteer put a drop of vinegar on each penny. The dark and dull film on the pennies should come off, resulting in bright, shiny pennies.

What do you think it means to have eternal life? *Pause for children to answer.* Eternal life, according to God, means that when you die, you will be able to be with him forever! Isn't that great?

Open your Bible to John 3:1-17, and show the page to children. In today's Bible story, we learn about a man who wanted to know how he could have eternal life. His name was Nicodemus.

Nicodemus knew Jesus came from God. He understood that Jesus could only do the miracles he did if God were with him. Jesus told Nicodemus that he could only see the kingdom of God if he were "born again."

What do you think it means to be "born again"? *Pause.* When the Bible talks about being "born again," it means that when someone believes in Jesus, he or she becomes a new person. What does it mean to become a new person? *Pause.* How does someone become a new person? *Pause.* When we become new people, it means that we've changed. And because we believe in Jesus and become new people, we can have eternal life.

Let's look at our Bible Verse for today to see what it says about having eternal life. *Open your Bible to John 3:16, and show the page to the children.* John 3:16 says, **"For God so loved the world that he gave his one and only Son, that whoever believes in him shall not perish but have eternal life."**

Let's take a look at our pennies and see what's happened to them. *Have kids go back to the tablecloth and have them each pick up a penny. Pass out moist paper towels and have kids wipe off the pennies.* What does your penny look like now? *Pause.* Why do you think the pennies changed? *Pause.*

Just like the solution we used got rid of the dark, dull stuff on these pennies, Jesus can take away the sin in your life when you believe in him. And that will make you a new person. You will be "born again."

The process for cleaning the pennies wasn't very hard. And neither is believing in Jesus. And the reward for believing in Jesus is not just having our sins forgiven, but also receiving eternal life!

 Let's pray right now. *Lead children in prayer. If appropriate, consider providing an opportunity for children to become followers of Jesus.* Dear God, thank you for loving us so much that you were willing to send your Son, Jesus, to die for our sins. Thank you that by believing in him, we can be born again and become new people and live forever with you. In Jesus' name, amen.

SECTION
THREE

SPRING
QUARTER

Jesus Talks With the Samaritan Woman

Bible Story: John 4:5-42

> **Bible Verse:** "He who has the Son has life; he who does not have the Son of God does not have life" (1 John 5:12).

Simple Supplies: *You'll need a Bible, a clean small plastic trash can, white grape juice, and paper cups. Before the service, empty the white grape juice into the trash can. Make sure you have enough juice so that children can fill their cups.*

L et's play pretend. Let's pretend that this trash can is a deep well from which people who lived in Jesus' time came to draw water. They didn't have running water in their homes as we do. They brought jars to the well, filled them with water, and carried them home for their drinking, cooking, and washing. Many people around the world still get their water this way, and they carry the jars of water home balanced on their heads. Why don't we try that now?

Give each child an empty cup and let them try to walk with the cups balanced on their heads.

That's even more difficult than it sounds. Now let's pretend that [name of an older female child] is a woman who's come to draw water from the well. Once Jesus met a woman at a well. He was waiting for his disciples to bring some food from the town, and she'd come to draw water.

She was surprised when Jesus talked to her and asked her for a drink, because she felt like no one cared about her. She was around people who wouldn't have anything to do with her. What might make someone feel like no one cares about him or her? *Pause for children to respond, and acknowledge that the things they mention might make someone feel left out.* The woman thought that she had two strikes against her because she was a woman and because she was from Samaria. She probably expected that Jesus would ignore her. But he didn't. Instead, Jesus told her all about her life. He talked with her about worshipping God, and he offered her living water—a relationship with God.

The woman at the well got a taste of God through her conversation with Jesus, and she got pretty excited about it. She ran back to town and told others about him.

Allow your "woman at the well" to fill her cup from the trash can and take a drink and then describe the "water" to the other children. Guide her with questions such as, "Why should others want a taste of this water?" and "How is this water different from other water you've tasted?" If she needs help, allow another child to take a drink and join her in convincing the others. Allow children to take a drink as they become convinced. Make sure every child who wants a drink gets one.

The woman at the well told people about Jesus, and they believed in him. Those people asked Jesus to stay with them, and many more people heard Jesus speak, and they believed in him too. What are some ways you can tell others about Jesus and his living water? *Respond to children's ideas enthusiastically.*

Open your Bible to 1 John 5:12, and show the page to the children. First John 5:12 says, **"He who has the Son has life; he who does not have the Son of God does not have life."** It's a great thing to have the life that comes from a relationship with God. And it's amazing that Jesus has given us the opportunity to tell others about him so that they can have life with God too. Let's thank God now.

Dear God, thanks for giving us life with you that is so much better than life without you. Thank you for letting us tell others about you also. In Jesus' name, amen.

Jesus Tells About the Good Samaritan
Bible Story: Luke 10:25-37

Bible Verse: "Be kind and compassionate to one another, forgiving each other, just as in Christ God forgave you" (Ephesians 4:32).

Simple Supplies: *You'll need a Bible, a box of brightly colored self-adhesive bandages, and a permanent marker. Write the words "I care about you" on enough bandages so that each child will have two.*

Give each child one bandage. Hello, children! Today we're going to talk about loving others, even when it's difficult. God loves all of us, and he wants

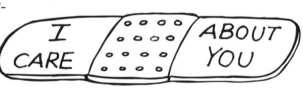

us to be like him. That means we should be kind to others.

I have given each of you a really cool-looking bandage. Why do we use bandages? *Pause for children's responses.* When we hurt ourselves, a bandage can make the bleeding stop and help us to feel better. But think for a moment. When you fall and scrape your knee or elbow, it really can hurt! What do you want to do right away? *Children will give a variety of responses; acknowledge each one positively.* Yes, I'll bet you want to run to someone who loves you so he or she can help you clean your "owie," put on a bandage on it, and give you a big hug. The best part about feeling hurt on the outside is getting that big hug, isn't it? Somehow love from others really can help take the pain away.

We can find in our Bible a verse that tells us to be kind and caring to one another. *Open your Bible to Ephesians 4:32, and show it to the children.* Ephesians 4:32 says, **"Be kind and compassionate to one another, forgiving each other, just as in Christ God forgave you."**

Jesus told of a man in the Bible who was robbed, beaten up, and left on the side of the road to die. Two people came down that road and just ignored the poor, injured man. How would you feel if you were ignored by others when you were hurt? *Pause for responses.* Yes, I'm sure I would feel hurt on the inside, too. But luckily, just as we have each other and our parents who care for us, finally someone came by and cared for this man who was so hurt. The kind person was a man from Samaria, and so he was known as a Samaritan, just as we are known as Americans. The good Samaritan cleaned the injured man's wounds, fed him, and took him to safety. And isn't this exactly what God would want all of us to do today? Yes! We must always be ready to help people who are hurting either on the outside or on the inside of their bodies.

I'm hoping each of us will remember to help others. To help you remember, I'd like you to put your special bandage on the person sitting next to you. *Help smaller children take the backings off of their bandages and direct the children so that everyone gets a bandage put on his or her arm or hand. Ask older children to collect the backings and throw them away.* Now tell your friend that you care for him or her. *Pause for the children to do this.*

That really was pretty easy, wasn't it? It's easy to show kindness to a friend. But remember, God wants us to help others whether we are their friends or not, just as the good Samaritan did. Sometimes we'll need to be kind to others even if we don't know them. *Begin to pass out another bandage to each child while you are talking.* So now I'm going to give each of you another bandage, and I'd like you to give it to someone sitting in the congregation who you don't really know very well. I'm sure that everyone sitting out there is going to smile when they see you coming toward them so it'll be easier for you. Right, congregation? *Smile at the congregation.* Now please go and give away your caring bandages and then come right back. *Give the children a few minutes to take their bandages out to the congregation. Encourage them and the congregation as they are doing this. Praise all for their efforts.*

Now that we're all back, let's say a little prayer to God. Dear Lord, help us to remember to be like you and always love and help others when they are in need of a friend. Thank you for loving us. In Jesus' name, amen.

Jesus Raises Lazarus from the Dead

Bible Story: John 11:1-45

> Bible Verse: "Jesus said to her, 'I am the resurrection and the life. He who believes in me will live, even though he dies' " (John 11:25).

Simple Supplies: *You'll need a Bible, one piece of facial tissue for each child, and a cup of water.*

Gather around me so I can tell you about Jesus' friends: Mary, Martha, and their brother Lazarus. *Pause while the children gather close to you.* One day Lazarus became very sick. The sisters knew Jesus could make their brother well again, but before Jesus got to their house, Lazarus died. Mary and Martha were so sad that their brother was gone. They must have cried as they buried Lazarus. *Dip your finger in the cup of water and place a drop of water like a tear on each child's cheek.* When have you been so sad that you cried? *Pause for children to respond.*

When Martha heard that Jesus was finally coming, she went to meet him and said, "Lord, if you had been here, my brother would not have died. But I know that even now God will give you whatever you ask."

Open your Bible to John 11:25, and show the page to the children. John 11:25 says, **"Jesus said to her, 'I am the resurrection and the life. He who believes in me will live, even though he dies.' "** Jesus wanted to give Martha hope. This verse tell us that everything was going to be OK because Jesus has power over death.

Jesus went to the tomb where Lazarus was buried. A tomb is a cave with a huge stone in front of it. Mary, Martha, and lots of friends were crying. Jesus cried too. Then Jesus prayed, thanking God for always hearing his prayers. When he finished praying, Jesus said in a loud voice, "Lazarus, come out!" Can you say that with me? *Lead children in repeating the phrase.* You know what? Lazarus came out of the tomb! Lazarus was alive and well again! Mary and Martha were no longer sad—they were happy! *Give each child a facial tissue and have them wipe away their "tears."*

Because of what Jesus did, lots of people believed in him. Jesus gave lots of people hope. What does it mean to have hope in God? *Pause for children to respond.* How can you have hope in God the next time you're sad? *Pause for children to respond.*

Let's say a prayer to our powerful, wonderful God. Dear God, help us hope in you the next time we are sad. *List the times the children told you earlier—times they've been so sad that they've cried.* Thank you that you have power over death. Thank you that we will live forever because of Jesus. Help us to always hope in you. In Jesus' name, amen. *Have children keep the facial tissues as reminders to always have hope in Jesus.*

Crowds Welcome Jesus to Jerusalem
Bible Story: Psalm 118:19-29; Matthew 21:1-11

> **Bible Verse:** "Worthy is the Lamb, who was slain, to receive power and wealth and wisdom and strength and honor and glory and praise!"(Revelation 5:12b).

Simple Supplies: *You'll need a Bible, balloons, and a helium tank (optional). You'll need one balloon for each child and a few extras.*

I f someone famous or important came into town to visit, how do you think that person would travel through town? *Pause for children's responses. Encourage their creativity by offering some outrageous suggestions, such as riding on a scooter or flying in a helicopter.* When Jesus lived on the earth, most of those things hadn't been invented yet. People walked or rode on animals to get places. Can you think of some animals that people might ride? *Pause for children's responses.*

Today we're going to hear about a special journey that Jesus took. *Open your Bible to Matthew 21:1-11, and show the page to the children.* Jesus had been teaching in the smaller towns and in the country for a while. He decided to go into the big city of Jerusalem. When he and his friends came to the edge of Jerusalem, Jesus told two of his disciples: "Go to the village ahead of you, and at once you will find a donkey tied there, with her colt by her. Untie them and bring them to me. If anyone says anything to you, tell him that the Lord needs them, and he will send them right away." What would you do if you saw something like this happening at your house or one of your neighbors' houses? *Pause for children's responses.* Jesus wasn't stealing the donkey and her colt; he was just going to borrow them so that he could fulfill an ancient prophecy about his life. His disciples brought the animals back and put their coats on the animals' backs. Then Jesus climbed on the colt to ride into the city. A big crowd had gathered there, and they put their coats on the road in front of the donkey. Some people broke branches from the palm trees and put some of them on the road and waved some of them as Jesus passed by. As Jesus rode along, the people were shouting. What would you shout if you saw Jesus riding into town? *Pause and let the children share what they might shout. For example, children may say, "Hooray!" "Yahoo!" or "Awesome!"* The people in Jerusalem shouted "Hosanna," which is a word that means "save." This is the way the people in Jerusalem showed that they were praising God and Jesus. At the beginning of the story, we thought about ways that we would welcome someone famous into town. Can you think of ways we might welcome Jesus to town today? *Pause and let the children share how we might welcome Jesus today, such as a parade or a TV appearance.* What would we say? *Pause and let the children shout their phrases that they thought of earlier.*

Open your Bible to Revelation 5:12b, and show the page to the children. Revelation 5:12b says, **"Worthy is the Lamb, who was slain, to receive power and wealth and wisdom and strength and honor and glory and praise!"** Who do you think the Lamb in this verse is? That's right, it's Jesus. One of the names for Jesus is "Lamb of God." This verse tells us that Jesus deserves our great praise because of who he is and what he does. What are some ways we can offer our praise to Jesus every day? *Pause for responses.*

Let's pray together. Dear God, thank you for sending your Son Jesus to save us. Help us to give him praise every day. In Jesus' name, amen.

The people in Jesus' time waved palm branches to show their praise and excitement; today we might wave balloons instead. I'm going to give each of you a balloon. As you leave, I'd like you to toss it in the air and shout the praise phrases you thought of earlier. *Give each child a balloon, and throw some extra balloons into the congregation.*

Jesus Rises from the Dead

Bible Story: Matthew 27:27-56; 28:1-10

Bible Verse: "I have been crucified with Christ and I no longer live, but Christ lives in me. The life I live in the body, I live by faith in the Son of God, who loved me and gave himself for me" (Galatians 2:20).

Simple Supplies: *You'll need a Bible and a bright lamp. Begin with the room lights slightly dimmed.*

We're going to hear a sad story that has a happy ending. Show me how you look when you're sad. *Pause for children to respond.* Next show me how you look when you're happy. *Pause for children to respond.* Well, the people who followed Jesus were very sad. Not everybody had wanted to hear Jesus tell about God. Some people hated Jesus. Now Jesus had died on a cross and was buried in a tomb. Early one day, two women went to see the tomb where Jesus was buried. Let's go with them to the tomb. *Have the children walk in place and then sit down.* How do you think they felt as they sat by the tomb where Jesus' body lay? *Pause for kids to respond.* Something happened that made them scared as well as sad. All of a sudden, there was an earthquake. An earthquake is when the ground shakes. *Have kids stomp their feet, move side to side, and look scared.* An angel of the Lord came who looked bright like lightning! *Turn on the bright light. Have kids stop stomping and then put their hands over their eyes as they look at the bright light.* The angel told them not to be afraid, because Jesus wasn't there in the tomb. The tomb was empty! Jesus had been raised from the dead, and they would see him soon. The women went to tell this good news to more of Jesus' followers. *Have kids walk in place.* On their way, Jesus met them! They bowed down at Jesus' feet and worshipped him. *Have everyone bow low.* Jesus told them not to be afraid but to go tell his followers that he'd see them soon. *Have kids sit down again.* Jesus had risen! He was alive! The women were so happy. When have you been so happy? *Pause for kids to respond.*

Open your Bible to Galatians 2:20, and show the page to the children. Galatians 2:20 says, **"I have been crucified with Christ and I no longer live, but Christ lives in me. The life I live in the body, I live by faith in the Son of God, who loved me and gave himself for me."** If we are Christians, Jesus lives in us. That means that what we say and do shows Jesus' love to others. If

Jesus lives in us, how should we talk? *Pause for kids to respond.* If Jesus lives in us, how should we act? *Pause for kids to respond.*

Let's say a prayer to thank God that Jesus is alive. Dear God, thank you that Jesus rose from the dead. Help us to tell others about you in all we say and do. In Jesus' name, amen.

Remember that if you're a Christian, Jesus lives in you. Show people Jesus' love in all you say and do.

Peter Explains Belief in Jesus

Bible Story: 1 Peter 1:3-9

> **Bible Verse:** "Not only so, but we also rejoice in our sufferings, because we know that suffering produces perseverance; perseverance, character; and character, hope" (Romans 5:3-4).

Simple Supplies: *You'll need a Bible; several hats that represent different occupations such as a fireman's helmet, a chef's hat, and a construction hard-hat; a bag or box; a very dirty penny; and a penny for each child.*

Ask for one volunteer at a time to pull a hat out of the bag, put it on, and then *describe the occupation of the person who would wear that hat.* Do any of you work? What kind of work do you do? What kind of work do you want to do when you are older? Why do you want to do that job? Why do you think people work? *Pause after each question for children to respond.*

One reason people work is to make money. In our society, we need money in order to have a place to live, clothes to wear, and food to eat. But we also like to have money for other things. If you had some money to spend, what would you buy? *Pause.*

Does anyone know what an inheritance is? *Pause.* An inheritance is money or special belongings that parents put aside for their children to have when they're adults. *Take out your dirty penny.* I have a penny here that could be part of someone's inheritance someday. *Pass the penny to a child and ask what he or she thinks of it.*

The problem with an inheritance is the problem with this penny. While you may someday receive a wonderful gift as an inheritance, over time money and belongings perish, spoil, or fade. This penny got really dirty. But in the Bible, Peter explains that you can have an inheritance that will never go bad: If you believe in Jesus, you can have the inheritance of hope.

Ask children to join hands as you take the hand of the child closest to you. Sometimes people talk about hope like this: "I hope I get the presents I want for my birthday" or "I hope you can come over after school tomorrow." That's OK. But when the Bible talks about hope, it means that we expect the future (in heaven with God) will be better than life on earth, as great as that is. Hope is the thing that makes us hold on tight *(visibly squeeze the hand you're holding)* to what we believe in even when it's hard. *Allow children to follow your example and squeeze each other's hands before letting go.*

Has anyone ever made fun of you for coming to church? *Pause.* If you believe in Jesus, you'll sometimes act differently from people you know, and they won't understand. They might want you to lie to your parents, or to cheat in school, or do other things you know are wrong. They might laugh at you for reading your Bible or for not joining in when they make fun of others. That's what was happening to the people Peter wrote to. But he encouraged them that they could praise God because of the hope they had in Jesus.

Open your Bible to Romans 5:3-4, and show the page to the children. Romans 5:3-4 says, **"Not only so, but we also rejoice in our sufferings, because we know that suffering produces perseverance; perseverance, character; and character, hope."**

Give each child a penny. Peter says you can praise God because of your inheritance of hope. Romans says you can rejoice in your sufferings because they, too, will lead to more hope. The great thing about this inheritance of hope is that you can have it right now. You don't need to wait for it, as you do for an inheritance of money.

Rejoicing as you suffer seems kind of backward, doesn't it? It'll take some practice. Let's practice rejoicing right now. Make a tight fist around your penny, hold it up, and when I count to three we'll shout, "Dear God, thanks for hope!" Got it? One, two, three:

Dear God, thanks for hope! In Jesus' name, amen.

Encourage children to put their pennies in their pockets so they can hold on to them and remember their inheritance of hope.

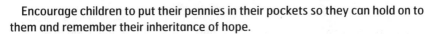

Jesus Returns to Heaven
Bible Story: Matthew 28:16-20; Acts 1:1-11

> **Bible Verse:** "Therefore go and make disciples of all nations, baptizing them in the name of the Father and of the Son and of the Holy Spirit, and teaching them to obey everything I have commanded you. And surely I am with you always, to the very end of the age" (Matthew 28:19-20).

Simple Supplies: *You'll need a Bible and a helium-filled balloon.*

Hey, I have some good news for you. Jesus loves you! Everyone say that with me. *Pause for children to respond.* Besides knowing that Jesus loves you, what else do you know about Jesus? *Pause for children to respond.* Jesus died and became alive again. For forty days, Jesus taught his followers many things. Before he left them, Jesus blessed his friends. Then Jesus went up into the sky, just like this balloon. *Release the helium-filled balloon.* We can still see the balloon above, but when Jesus went up, clouds hid him. His friends stood looking up for a long time. Then angels stood by them and told them that Jesus had gone to heaven and someday he'd come back the same way they saw him leave. Everyone was so happy that Jesus was alive and that he taught them so many things.

 Before Jesus went to heaven, he told his friends an important message. *Open your Bible to Matthew 28:19-20, and show the page to the children.* Matthew 28:19-20 says, **"Therefore go and make disciples of all nations, baptizing them in the name of the Father and of the Son and of the Holy Spirit, and teaching them to obey everything I have commanded you. And surely I am with you always, to the very end of the age."**

 God helps us tell others about Jesus. Let's pray, asking God to help us spread the good news of Jesus' love. Dear God, please help us tell others about Jesus so all people in the world will know how much you love them. In Jesus' name, amen.

God helps us tell others about Jesus. I'd like you to think for a moment about who you can tell about Jesus when you go home. Maybe you can tell a friend or a neighbor or a family member. *Allow time for kids to think.* Has everyone thought of someone to tell about Jesus? Let's see what spreading the good news of Jesus' love looks like. *Tell two children "Jesus loves you. Spread the news!" When you tell them, have them stand. Then have them each tell two more kids the good news, and have them stand. Have kids continue until all the children are standing, then have the last kids go to the congregation and tell others. Continue until everyone in the entire congregation is standing.*

Look at how many people have heard about Jesus! Throughout today and the rest of your lives, remember to spread the news to your family, friends, kids at school, and the whole world. Jesus loves you!

Christians Care for One Another
Bible Story: Psalm 23; Acts 2:42-47

 Bible Verse: "And let us consider how we may spur one another on toward love and good deeds. Let us not give up meeting together, as some are in the habit of doing, but let us encourage one another—and all the more as you see the Day approaching" (Hebrews 10:24-25).

Simple Supplies: *You'll need a Bible, a large pointer (you can make an arrow from plastic foam, use a foam "finger" from a sports team, or use a blackboard pointer), and two craft sticks and one chenille wire for each child.*

U*sing the pointer, call on children at random to answer the following questions, pausing for their responses. You can ask each question more than once.*

What's one thing you like about your family? What do you enjoy doing with your friends? Why do you like to come to church? Share with us one thing you like about a good friend. How do your parents show that they love you?

You've got some great family members and friends. I like to spend time with my family and friends too. *Share one or two things you enjoy doing with others.* Spending time with people who care about you is important. They're the people who make you feel good about being yourself, and they're the ones who will let you know when you're not doing so well.

After Jesus rose from the dead and went up into heaven, his followers spent a lot of time together. The Bible tells us in Acts 2 that they ate together, prayed and praised God together, listened while the apostles taught them about Jesus and what it meant to be his follower, and they shared what they had in order to take care of each other's needs. They spent time together because they really enjoyed being together.

Before we continue, let's follow the example of the early church and praise God for the people he's put in our church. I'll begin by saying, "Dear God, we praise you for..." and you fill in people's names—your parents, your friends, your Sunday school teachers, and others you want to thank God for. Ready? Let's pray.

Dear God, we praise you for _____. In Jesus' name, amen.

Thank you for praying with me. We've got lots of people in our church to thank God for. Church should be a place where people who follow Jesus come together to worship God and love each other. What else could we do to show others that we care about them? *Pause for responses.*

Open your Bible to Hebrews 10:24-25, and show the page to the children. Hebrews 10:24-25 says, **"And let us consider how we may spur one another on toward love and good deeds. Let us not give up meeting together, as some are in the habit of doing, but let us encourage one another—and all the more as you see the Day approaching."**

Give each child two craft sticks and one chenille wire. This verse says we should "spur" each other to love and good deeds. That means we point each other to the things we need to do to care for each other. Look around the room at all the people gathered here. *Pause while children scan the room.* God has brought together so many different people! But there's one thing we have in common: We're here because of Jesus. Jesus holds people in the church together. Let's make a pointer to remind us that we can care for others in our church by pointing them to love and good deeds because Jesus has gathered us together.

Hold the craft sticks together in the middle so they form a plus sign and wrap the chenille wire around the intersection of the sticks. Hold one end of the wire under your thumb on the intersection of the sticks. Wrap behind the intersection on one stick, then around the front again (across the held end of the wire) and down to the opposite angle. Wrap behind the same stick on the other side of the intersection and around the front again so that you have an X across the end of the wire you held with your thumb. Continue wrapping until you've used up the length of the wire and then tuck the end under. Hold the craft sticks up so children can see how you wrap them. Encourage older children to help younger ones.

The people in our church are like your craft sticks. Jesus is like the wire, holding the people in the church together. You can use your pointer to remember that you can point others to the importance of spending time with other Christians.

Stephen Forgives His Accusers as They Stone Him
Bible Story: Acts 6:8–7:60

> **Bible Verse:** "But in your hearts set apart Christ as Lord. Always be prepared to give an answer to everyone who asks you to give the reason for the hope that you have. But do this with gentleness and respect" (1 Peter 3:15).

Simple Supplies: *You'll need a Bible, modeling clay, and pencils.*

What does it mean to share our faith? *Pause for children to answer.* Sharing our faith simply means that we tell other people about Jesus.

How should we share our faith? *Pause.* Let's take a look at a man in the Bible who shared his faith.

Open your Bible to Acts 6:8—7:60, and show the page to the kids. In today's Bible story, we learn about a man named Stephen who loved God very much and was always telling other people about Jesus.

Have kids stand and form two circles. One circle should be inside the other; kids in the outer circle should be facing inward, and kids in the inner circle should be facing outward.

Have children each share one thing they know about Jesus with the child standing in front of him or her. Then have children rotate to their right. Each time they rotate, they will share something they know about Jesus. They can repeat the same thing over and over again, or they can share something new they've learned from one of the other children. You may want to give them some suggestions, such as, "Jesus is God's Son," Jesus loves me," "Jesus loves you," or "Jesus is awesome!" Once children have spoken to several other children, have them sit down.

How did it feel to tell others what you know about Jesus? *Pause.* Do you think you could tell your friends at school about Jesus? Why or why not? *Pause.*

I told you that today's Bible story is about a man named Stephen. Stephen was a man who wasn't afraid to do what was right, even when lots of other people disagreed with him. He wasn't afraid to do what was right when other people lied about him. And that's exactly what happened. There were some people who didn't like what Stephen was saying about Jesus. They accused him of blasphemy, which means saying things about God that are not true.

So these people had Stephen arrested and taken to the officials, called the Sanhedrin. Have you ever had anyone get mad at you for talking about Jesus? *Pause and allow those children with stories to share them.*

The Sanhedrin questioned Stephen about the things he was saying, and he told them about all the great things God had done for his people in the past. He talked about Abraham, Isaac, Jacob, Joseph, Moses, and David.

But then Stephen called the Sanhedrin stubborn and rebellious. He told them that they opposed the Holy Spirit and hurt prophets who talked about Jesus coming. Then he told them that they were disobedient to God and murdered Jesus, the "Righteous One."

The men of the Sanhedrin were very angry with Stephen, and they began to throw stones at him to kill him. *Give each child a piece of modeling clay and a pencil. Have each child form the modeling clay into the shape of a smooth stone. Then have children each use a pencil to carve the word "SHARE" on one side of the stone and "JESUS" on the other side. You may want to have the older children help the younger children with the writing.*

But do you know what Stephen did? He did the very same thing Jesus did: He forgave them! He said "Lord, do not hold this sin against them" right before he died.

Open your Bible to 1 Peter 3:15, and show the page to the children. First Peter 3:15 says, **"But in your hearts set apart Christ as Lord. Always be prepared to give an answer to everyone who asks you to give the reason for the hope that you have. But do this with gentleness and respect."** This verse tells us that we should always be ready to share Jesus with others, no matter what. I'd like you to take your stones home as a reminder to share Jesus with everyone you meet.

Let's pray right now. *Lead children in prayer.*

Dear God, thank you for Jesus. Help us always to be ready to share what we believe about Jesus with other people. In Jesus' name, amen.

Paul Teaches in Athens

Bible Story: Acts 17:16-31

> **Bible Verse: "Do you not know? Have you not heard? The Lord is the everlasting God, the Creator of the ends of the earth" (Isaiah 40:28a).**

Simple Supplies: *You'll need a Bible, a picture of Jesus, a towel, a sheet of paper, and a marker. Cover the picture with the towel. Draw a question mark on the paper and place it on top of the towel.*

Gather the children around the towel. Right now, you don't know what's under this towel—it's unknown. But go ahead and guess. *Have children guess what's underneath the towel, but don't tell them what it is.* You have lots of ideas and questions about what's under this towel. In a minute I'll tell you all about it. Right now I'll tell you about one of Jesus' followers named Paul. He went to a city to tell people about Jesus. When he got to the city, he found out that the people were worshipping and praying to fake gods. They didn't know about the one true God. Paul noticed that they had a sign that was kind of like this. *Motion toward the towel and the question mark.* The sign said "To an unknown god." Paul told the people that our one true God made the world and everything in it. He said that we are God's children and God made us alive. If you were with Paul, what else would you have told the people about God? *Pause for children to respond.* Paul told the people all of these things and helped them know about the one true God. *Take the towel off of the picture of Jesus and let everyone see it.* Jesus is Lord of heaven and earth. Jesus is alive. He is the one true God.

The Bible helps us know all about the one true God. *Open your Bible to Isaiah 40:28a, and show children the page.* Isaiah 40:28a says, **"Do you not know? Have you not heard? The Lord is the everlasting God, the Creator of the ends of the earth."**

Everybody take a moment and tell someone sitting close to you everything you know about God. *Pause for children to share.* When you go home today, tell your family and friends everything you know about God too. God wants us to tell everyone all about him and how much he loves us.

Let's pray and thank God for all he is and does. Dear God, thank you for making yourself known to us through the Bible, church, and Christians. Thanks for creating us and everything around us. Help us tell others that you are our living God and you created all things. In Jesus' name, amen.

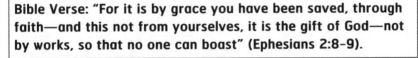

Paul Explains Christians' Relationship With Christ

Bible Story: Ephesians 1:15–2:10

> **Bible Verse:** "For it is by grace you have been saved, through faith—and this not from yourselves, it is the gift of God—not by works, so that no one can boast" (Ephesians 2:8-9).

Simple Supplies: *You'll need a Bible, a helmet, and a piece of wrapped candy for each child.*

'm going to begin today by telling you a story. Grant wanted to ride his new scooter. His father wouldn't let him until he had a helmet. But helmets cost twenty dollars and Grant only had ten dollars. He tried to earn the money. He raked leaves for his neighbor. He walked his aunt's dog. He even sold one of his shark's teeth to a little boy down the street, but Grant still didn't have enough money to buy a helmet.

Grant was discouraged. He sat by the road watching all the other kids zip by on their scooters. Just then, Sara, his twin sister, whizzed by on her roller blades. She stopped. She took off her helmet and placed it on Grant's head. *Take out the helmet and set it among the children.* "Wow! Thanks!" Grant said. "Let me pay you the seventeen dollars I've earned."

"No," said Sara. "Just take it. Wear it. It can protect you. It's a gift." Grant raced off with the helmet on. He had a blast whirling around on his scooter. Grant never saw the truck behind him as he darted across the street without looking. Crash! Grant flew off the scooter and lay in the street. He had been knocked out.

An ambulance took him to the hospital. The doctor looked at Grant and the cracked helmet and said, "You would be dead if it weren't for that helmet. That helmet saved your life." As Grant recovered, he felt as if he had been saved by a sweet, unseen hand from certain death.

Why did Grant's sister, Sara, give him her helmet? *Pause*. What did Grant do to earn the helmet from her? *Pause*.

Open your Bible to Ephesians 2:8-9, and show the page to the children. Ephesians 2:8-9 says, **"For it is by grace you have been saved, through faith—and this not from yourselves, it is the gift of God—not by works, so that no one can boast."** This means that when God saves us, it is a kind act, a free favor.

Hand each child a piece of candy. Did you have to behave during the message to get that piece of candy? No. Did you have to pay me for it? No. What did you have to do to earn that candy from me? *Pause*. The candy was simply a gift. Jesus' forgiveness is God's gift to us. Jesus died to save us. His broken body became like our helmet, saving us. God loved us so much that even though we were like dead because of our sins, he gave us back our lives again when he raised Christ from the dead. It is only because of what *he* did, not because of anything good *we* do that he lifts us up from the grave. Because of his kindness, you have been saved through trusting Christ. And even your trusting is not your own, it too is a gift from God. We can't take any credit for God's saving us and bringing us to heaven. It is by grace you have been saved through faith.

Let's pray together. Dear God, thank you for being the hand that caught me. You reached out and saved me, dear Jesus. You became the cracked and broken helmet, taking what I deserved upon yourself, being wounded for my sins. You died on the cross so I could live. Thank you. Thank you for giving me this free gift that I can't earn. I can't buy it. I can't do enough good things to make up for it. All I can do is take it as a gift. Thank you. In Jesus' name, amen.

Paul comforts Others in a Storm
Bible Story: Acts 27:1-44

> **Bible Verse: "In everything set them an example by doing what is good" (Titus 2:7a).**

Simple Supplies: *You'll need a Bible and a loaf of unsliced bread.*

Form two groups of children. Tell one group that every time you say "wind," they should shout "Whoosh!" Tell the other group that every time you say, "storm," they should shout "Boom! Crash!"

I'm going to read a story, and I want you to help create some dramatic effects. Listen carefully and say your lines each time I say "wind" *(pause for children to respond)* or "storm" *(pause)*. Good! You got it. Let's begin.

The Apostle Paul had been arrested for talking about Jesus too much. His accusers put him on a ship headed for Rome where he would stand trial. The wind *(pause)* made it difficult to sail. Paul warned the sailors that it was a dangerous season for sailing, but they didn't listen to him.

A gentle wind *(pause)* began to blow, so the sailors thought they were right to keep going. But before long, the wind *(pause)* became a hurricane. The ship was caught by the storm *(pause)* and couldn't head into the wind *(pause)*. The storm *(pause)* battered the ship and the crew began to throw cargo overboard. The storm *(pause)* raged for three days, during which the people on the ship couldn't see the sun or the moon and they lost all hope of being saved.

Paul said, "Keep up your courage! An angel of God told me that we will all live through this windy *(pause)* storm *(pause)*."

The wind *(pause)* and storm *(pause)* continued for fourteen days. No one ate any *food because they fought against the* storm (pause). Paul urged them to eat, saying, "You need food to survive. The storm (pause) won't hurt you." And he gave thanks to God and ate in front of them. So they all ate until they were full.

In the morning they saw an island and tried to use the wind (pause) to get to the beach. The boat crashed and the people had to swim, but everyone reached land in safety, just as God had promised Paul. Applaud children's dramatic participation.

How do you think the people on the boat felt after two weeks of storm and no food? *Pause for children to respond.* I imagine they felt pretty scared and discouraged. Can someone share a time when they felt scared or sad? Pause and then thank anyone who shares. We all get discouraged sometimes and need people like Paul to cheer us up. Other times we need to be like Paul and encourage people we know. What are some ways you can comfort others? *Pause.* What great ideas!

Open your Bible to Titus 2:7a, and show the page to the children. Titus 2:7a says, **"In everything set them an example by doing what is good."**

Paul did good by encouraging others on the ship, but he also did good by eating, since everyone needed food. One way you can encourage others is by giving them an example to follow. I have a loaf of bread here. I'm going to tear off a piece and say that I can be an example for others by telling people about Jesus. *Give children other examples such as being kind, helping around the house, helping a friend, and telling the truth.*

What other good things can you do to set an example for others? As you tear off a piece of bread, tell us what you can do. *Pass around the loaf of bread. Don't pressure any child to speak, but make sure everyone gets a piece of bread who wants one.*

You have great ideas about what it means to do good. Now let's ask God to help us be good examples. Dear God, help us to do good so that others will follow you too. In Jesus' name, amen.

Paul Describes Genuine Love

Bible Story: 1 Corinthians 13:1-13

Bible Verse: "Love is patient, love is kind. It does not envy, it does not boast, it is not proud. It is not rude, it is not self-seeking, it is not easily angered, it keeps no record of wrongs" (1 Corinthians 13:4-5).

Simple Supplies: *You'll need a Bible.*

What would you think of me if I could speak every language? *Pause after each question for responses.* How about if I knew what would happen in the future? What if I could tell mountains to move and they did? What would you think if I gave everything I own to the poor? How about this: What if I could do all those things, but I was the meanest person to ever live? *Pause.*

The Bible says that even if I could do those things, I wouldn't be anything special if I didn't have love. The Bible also says that those abilities will stop, but love never fails. Apparently love is pretty important. So, what's love? *Let children attempt to define love.* You have some good ideas about what love means. Let's hear what the Bible has to say.

Open your Bible to 1 Corinthians 13:4-5, and show the page to the children. First Corinthians 13:4-5 says, **"Love is patient, love is kind. It does not envy, it does not boast, it is not proud. It is not rude, it is not self-seeking, it is not easily angered, it keeps no record of wrongs."** These verses point to something pretty important: You love someone by how you act.

First the Bible says, "Love is patient." What does it mean to be patient? *Pause.* Great! Someone who isn't patient is always in a hurry. They miss what's going on right now, right in front of them. Love says, "Slow down! Enjoy this." To help us remember to slow down, do this hand motion with me—put your hand on your wrist, as if you're covering up your watch. *Pause for children to follow, and affirm their participation.*

Next the Bible says, "Love is kind." How can you show someone kindness? *Pause for responses.* I'm sure you are all very kind. But sometimes you might feel tempted to push someone out of your way. To remember to be kind, do this— stroke the back of your hand gently, as if you're petting a dog. *Pause.*

Review the hand motion for patience, then for kindness.

The Bible says that love does not envy. When you envy someone, you become jealous of the things they have. Can you think of a time when you felt jealous? What were you jealous of? *Pause*. We all get jealous, but the feeling of envy gets in the way of loving others. To remember not to envy, let's put our hands over our eyes. *Pause*.

The Bible also says that love doesn't boast and it's not proud. Not boasting means you don't tell others how great you are. Not being proud means you don't think about how great you are. Now, that doesn't mean you aren't great. God has made each of you very special, and he wants to do great things through you. But if you're too busy talking or thinking about yourself, then you won't be loving others. To remember not to boast, put your hands over your mouth. *Pause*. To remember to not be proud, let's get on our knees. *With children on their knees, review all hand motions.*

We're sure learning a lot about love today! Next the Bible says that love is not rude. What kinds of rude things do people do to each other? *Pause*. How do you feel when someone is rude to you? *Pause*. You don't feel loved by them, do you? So to show love for others, we need to remember not to be rude. Why don't you stand and take the hands of the people next to you? *Pause*.

Love is not self-seeking. People who are self-seeking want things for themselves. What kind of hand motion would show that? *Pause*. You're right. Self-seeking looks like taking, grabbing, and holding. If you're not self-seeking, though, you might be giving things (or yourself!) away. Let's hold out our hands with the palms up to show that love is not self-seeking. *Pause*.

Only two more. The Bible says that love is not easily angered. What makes you feel angry? *Pause*. Lots of things can make us angry. But if we get angry all the time, we won't have many friends. Why? Because we won't be showing love for them by forgiving them. Have your parents ever told you to count to ten when you feel angry so you have time to cool off before you say something you don't mean? Let's count to ten on our fingers to remember not to be easily angered. *Count to ten with the children.*

Finally, the Bible says that love keeps no record of wrongs. Pretend you have a piece of paper in front of your face. This is the list you've been making of things that bother you about other people. Let's tear it up *(pretend to tear the imaginary piece of paper)*. Now there's nothing standing in the way of you loving others.

Read 1 Corinthians 13:4-5 again, coaching children in the hand motions. Lead the congregation in applause for the children.

Let's thank God that he's told us how to love others. Dear God, thank you for loving us and teaching us how to love others. In Jesus' name, amen.

SECTION

FOUR

SUMMER

QUARTER

Elisha Helps a Widow and Her Sons

Bible Story: 2 Kings 4:1-7

> **Bible Verse:** "He defends the cause of the fatherless and the widow, and loves the alien, giving him food and clothing" (Deuteronomy 10:18).

Simple Supplies: *You'll need a Bible, small paper cups, and a medicine dropper filled with water. Give each person in the congregation a small paper cup, and tell them to hold onto the cups until the children ask for them.*

What are some of the things that you need? *Pause for children to answer.* Who gives you the things you need? *Pause.* Most of you get the things you need, such as a place to live, food, and clothing, from your parents. But who do you think would give you those things if you didn't have your parents to give them to you?

In today's Bible story, we'll hear about a woman whose husband died, making her a widow. This also meant that her two boys didn't have a father anymore. Let's listen to their story. *Open your Bible to 2 Kings 4:1-7, and show the passage to the children.*

The widow and her two sons were probably very sad that this man, who loved God, had died. I want you to show me your saddest faces. *Pause for children to show you their saddest faces.* But to make matters worse, there were people who wanted money from the woman, and they were coming to take her sons away to be slaves! What do you think the woman should have done? *Pause.* Well, she turned to Elisha, the prophet, and told him her story.

Elisha asked her how he could help. What do you think Elisha did? *Pause.* You might think Elisha offered to give her money to pay her debts, or offered to buy her food and clothing, but that's not what he did. Instead, Elisha told the woman to go and collect empty jars from all of her neighbors.

Like the widow, I want you to go and collect empty cups from the adults in our service today. You just need to go up to as many adults as you can in one minute and ask them for the empty cups. *Give children one minute to collect as many cups as they can, and then have them come back and sit down.*

Wow! Look at all of the cups you found! Now let's find out what happened in our story. Elisha told the widow to fill all of the jars with oil. The widow agreed to do what Elisha told her to do, even though she only had a little bit of oil. It would be like trying to fill all of your empty cups with water using only a medicine dropper. *Have kids pass around the medicine dropper full of water and try to fill their cups.*

We weren't able to fill all of our cups, but the widow was able to fill all of her jars. How do you think she was able to fill all those jars with just a little bit of oil? *Pause.*

76

God did something miraculous for the widow. He allowed all of her jars to be filled, and once they were filled, the oil stopped flowing. How do you think the widow felt when she saw that she was able to fill all of the jars with just the little bit of oil she had? *Pause.*

Elisha told the widow to sell the oil and pay her debts and then live on what was left. How did God take care of the widow's needs? *Pause.* How does God take care of our needs? *Pause.*

Let's take a look at our Bible verse for today and see what it says. *Open your Bible to Deuteronomy 10:18, and show the page to the children.* Deuteronomy 10:18 says, **"He defends the cause of the fatherless and the widow, and loves the alien, giving him food and clothing."** Do you think this verse means God will take care of you? Why or why not? *Pause.* This verse means that God will take care of everyone, even widows, orphans, and aliens—people who are from other places. God loves each and every one of us so much that he will take care of us even when the situation may seem impossible. How does God take care of you? *Pause.* How have you seen God take care of other people? *Pause.*

Let's thank God right now for all he does for us.

Dear Lord, thank you for caring so much about us! Help us to remember that whenever we need something, we can ask you and you'll take care of us. In Jesus' name we pray, amen.

God Heals Naaman's Leprosy

Bible Story: 2 Kings 5:1-16

> **Bible Verse:** "Humble yourselves, therefore, under God's mighty hand, that he may lift you up in due time" (1 Peter 5:6).

Simple Supplies: *You'll need a Bible.*

B*egin by pairing older children with younger children.*

I'd like you to talk to your partner and think together of something really big, like a bear, and then try to make your bodies look that big. For example, if you choose a bear, you could stand on your tippy-toes with your arms up and "claws" out and snarl at us. *Model this for the children and then give pairs a minute to discuss and assume their postures. Ask each pair what they represent.*

God made some pretty big things, many of which are a lot bigger than people. But sometimes people think they're bigger than they really are. Can you think of some really important people? *Pause after each question for responses.* What makes them important? What kinds of important things would you like to do with your life?

God can use each of you to do important things. You might discover the cure for a disease or start an organization that helps people. I hope you will love people that God brings into your lives, and tell them about Jesus. These are all important things. But you'll get into trouble if you start to think that you're bigger—or more important—than you are.

Second Kings 5 tells us about someone who had that problem. Naaman had a really important job: He commanded the army of the king of Aram. The king—the most important guy around—thought Naaman was pretty big stuff. His position as commander and the king's appreciation of him made Naaman feel bigger than he was.

But Naaman had a skin disease called leprosy. He heard that a prophet in Samaria could cure him. So the king of Aram sent a letter to the king of Israel, asking that Naaman be cured. The king of Israel—as important as he was—despaired, because he knew that only God held the power of life and death. But Elisha, a prophet of God, sent for Naaman.

Elisha told Naaman to go wash in the river seven times and God would cure him. If you had been Naaman, would you go swimming and let God cure you? *Pause.* Naaman didn't. He got angry and left. He thought he was such a big guy that Elisha should do a great miracle for him, or at least tell him to go wash in a great river, not just some ordinary river.

Now I'd like you to talk to your partner and think together of something really small and try to make your bodies look that small. *Give children a minute to assume their postures and then ask each pair what they represent.*

We can learn something from these little guys. God made them important, but not big. Just like people. God made you, and so you are important. You can do important things for God. But it helps to remember that you are still a little guy, not too big to do little things.

Open your Bible to 1 Peter 5:6, and show the page to the children. First Peter 5:6 says, **"Humble yourselves, therefore, under God's mighty hand, that he may lift you up in due time."**

Being humble means that you remember you're a little guy. Even all those big guys out there in the congregation, even though they may do really important things, they're still little guys next to God. Naaman's friends helped him remember to be a little guy, so he washed himself in the river and God healed him. And Naaman worshipped God. Let's pray to God now.

Dear God, thanks for making us little guys so that you can take care of us. Help us to always remember that we're special and important to you, even though we are just little guys. In Jesus' name, amen.

Jonah Learns a Lesson

Bible Story: Jonah 1:1–3:10

Bible Verse: "The ways of the Lord are right; the righteous walk in them, but the rebellious stumble in them" (Hosea 14:9b).

Simple Supplies: *You'll need a Bible, a blue sheet, a spray bottle filled with water, and a blanket.*

Today we're going to learn about Jonah and how he found out that God's ways are best. You'll all have a part to play in this story. *Choose someone to be Jonah, three kids to be sailors, two kids to hold the blue sheet to be the "water," one kid to be the king of Nineveh, and the rest of the kids to stand in a line behind the sheet to do the "wave" when the storm hits and to play the role of the Ninevites at the end of the story.*

One day, God told Jonah, "Go to a city called Nineveh. Tell the people to stop the bad things they're doing." Jonah didn't want to do it. *Have Jonah cross his arms and shake his head "no."* Instead of going to Nineveh, Jonah did the opposite of what God wanted him to do. Jonah ran away to the sea and got on a ship. *Have the two kids hold the blue sheet and move it gently up and down. Have the three sailors stand behind the sheet and pretend to row the boat. Have Jonah join in rowing.* At first the water was calm. *Have the two kids gently move the sheet. Have the other kids do a very calm wave. Starting at one end of the line, have them calmly and slowly stand, raise their hands over their heads, lower their hands, and then sit back down.* Then the storm got worse and the waves got higher. *Have kids make their water and wave get bigger.* Then the storm got so bad, the waves were huge. *Have kids make their water and wave as big as possible. Spray everyone with the spray bottle.* Jonah told the sailors that the storm had come because of him. He said, "Throw me in the water and the storm will stop." *Have Jonah and the sailors pretend to talk.* So the sailors threw Jonah in the sea. *Have the sailors gently take Jonah and put him out of the boat on the opposite side of the sheet. Have the water and the waves become calm and have Jonah pretend to swim.* God sent a big fish and it swallowed Jonah. *Throw the blanket over Jonah.* Inside the fish Jonah prayed and prayed. After three days and nights, God saved

Jonah. God had the fish spit Jonah out on land. *Take the blanket off Jonah and have him stand and wave.* Then God said, "Jonah, really, I mean it. Go to Nineveh!" And Jonah went. *Have Jonah wave goodbye to the sailors and sea. Have the "wave" people become the Ninevites.* Jonah told the people to stop doing bad things. They listened to Jonah and started doing good things. Jonah learned that God's ways are best. *Have all the actors take a bow.* Good job, actors!

How do you think Jonah felt when he was swallowed by a big fish? *Pause for children to respond.* How do you think Jonah felt when God saved him? *Pause for children to respond. Open your Bible to Hosea 14:9b, and show the page to* the children. Hosea 14:9b says, **"The ways of the Lord are right; the righteous walk in them, but the rebellious stumble in them."** It took Jonah awhile to learn that the ways of the Lord are right. But Jonah finally did what God wanted. What do you think it means to follow God's directions? *Pause for children to respond.* How do we know what God wants us to do in our lives? *Pause for children to respond.* Hearing Bible stories, listening to other Christians, going to Sunday school and church, and praying are all ways you can know God's directions for your life. God loves you so much and wants you to tell others, too.

Let's thank God for Jonah and the lesson he taught us. Dear God, thanks for Jonah and for helping him do what you wanted. Help us do what you want too. We know that your ways are the best for our lives. In Jesus' name, amen.

Jonah Complains About God's Compassion

Bible Story: Jonah 3:10–4:11

> **Bible Verse:** "The Lord is not slow in keeping his promise, as some understand slowness. He is patient with you, not wanting anyone to perish, but everyone to come to repentance" (2 Peter 3:9).

Simple Supplies: *You'll need a Bible.*

Let's play a game kind of like Simon Says. I'll tell you something to do, but I don't want you to do it unless I say "quick" or "slow." For example, if I said, "Do a jumping jack," you wouldn't move. If I said, "Do a quick jumping jack," then you would do a jumping jack as fast as you can. If I said, "Take three slow steps," you would take three very slow steps. Got it? Let's play.

Following is a list of motions to which you may or may not add "quick" or "slow." You can vary the suggested number of times children do each motion or add your own motions if time allows. This game is not for competition. Allow everyone to continue to play even if they get one wrong.

Hop on one foot.

Do a jumping jack.

Wave at the congregation.

Pat your head.

Take three steps forward.

Spin around.

Wiggle your body.

Clap your hands.

Lead the congregation in a round of applause for the children.

Sometimes you need to do things quickly, and other times it's important to move slowly. Can you give me an example of something you need to do quickly? *Pause for responses.* How about slowly? *Pause.* If you're running a race, it's a good idea to move quickly. But if you're trying to sneak up quietly on someone to surprise him or her, you probably want to move slowly. You don't want to mix up when you should be quick or slow.

But the Bible tells us that Jonah got mixed up. God asked him to go tell the people of Nineveh to stop doing wrong. Jonah should have been quick to obey God. Instead, he was quick to run away. Jonah didn't like the people of Nineveh, and he wanted God to be quick to be angry with them. But instead, God is slow to anger and quick to love. God showed compassion to the people of Nineveh who didn't know him. What does compassion mean? *Pause for responses.* When someone shows compassion to someone else, it means that he or she actively cares for that person and wants to help him or her. When you are compassionate with someone, it means that you are slow to show anger and quick to show love.

God was slow to become angry with the people of Nineveh, and quick to love and forgive them when they turned away from their sins and to him, and God wanted Jonah to show them the same compassion.

Open your Bible to 2 Peter 3:9, and show the page to the children. Second Peter 3:9 says, **"The Lord is not slow in keeping his promise, as some understand slowness. He is patient with you, not wanting anyone to perish, but everyone to come to repentance."**

Sometimes we, like Jonah, get our quick and our slow mixed up. We sometimes think God moves too slowly, when really he's waiting for people to turn to him. We need to learn from God to be quick to love and slow to be angry. God can show us how to be compassionate to everyone, especially people who don't know him or do what he wants them to do. What are some ways you can show compassion to people who don't know God? *Pause.* Great ideas! I'd like you to choose one of those ideas and try to do it this week. Remember that God wants you to be slow to get angry and quick to love everyone, even people who don't know him. Let's pray together.

Dear God, thank you for loving us so much that you show us compassion when we turn away from you. Help us to share your compassion with other people. In Jesus' name, amen.

God Calls Isaiah

Bible Story: Isaiah 6:1-8

> **Bible Verse: "Come, let us bow down in worship, let us kneel before the Lord our Maker" (Psalm 95:6).**

Simple Supplies: *You'll need a Bible.*

I want to tell about a prophet of God named Isaiah. Do any of you know what a prophet is? *Pause for children to respond.* A prophet is a special person God uses to tell other people about God. One day, Isaiah was in the temple, God's special home. Something happened to Isaiah that forever changed his life.

He saw God! He really saw God!

Isaiah saw God seated high upon a throne. Above him were special flying creatures with six wings. The creatures kept saying, "Holy, holy, holy is the Lord Almighty; the whole earth is full of his glory."

When Isaiah saw God's holiness, he worshipped God. Psalm 95:6 says, **"Come, let us bow down in worship, let us kneel before the Lord our Maker."**

After Isaiah worshipped God, God asked Isaiah a very important question.

God asked Isaiah, "Whom shall I send? And who will go for us?" And Isaiah said, "Here Am I. Send Me!"

I'm going to ask you the same question God asked the prophet Isaiah. After I ask it, I want you to answer, "Here I am. Send me!" *Ask the question.* Can you tell me something you know about God or Jesus? *Pause for children to respond. Ask the question, "who will I send to tell others about God?" After children respond, send them out to the people in the congregation with their message. If children didn't share a message, have them use, "God loves you," for their message. After the children have shared their messages, have them rejoin you.*

Dear God, thank you for loving us. Thank you for helping us share your love with others. Help us to be able to say to you always, "Here I am. Send me!" In Jesus' name, amen.

Josiah Promises to follow the Lord

Bible Story: 2 Chronicles 34:1-33

> **Bible Verse:** "All Scripture is God-breathed and is useful for teaching, rebuking, correcting and training in righteousness, so that the man of God may be thoroughly equipped for every good work" (2 Timothy 3:16-17).

Simple Supplies: *You'll need a Bible.*

We're going to play a game. I'll read a statement, and I want you to do the motion you think most fits that statement. You need to remember four motions. If I say something that you need to *know*, tap your finger to your head, like this. *Do the motion and encourage children to imitate you.* Great! If I say something that you should *stop*, hold your arm out straight with your hand up, like this. *Again, demonstrate for the children.* If the statement indicates something you need to *change*, turn your whole body to the right. *Have children turn so they face the right side of your church.* If I say something that you need to *do*, pump your arms back and forth like this—*demonstrate the motion*—as if you're running. *Review the four motions.* More than one motion might fit each statement, so just choose the one you think fits best. Got it? Let's begin.

Read the following statements, pausing after each one for children to respond. Ask children who choose different responses why they chose that motion.

Don't talk to strangers.

Look both ways before you cross the street.

Brush your teeth after you eat.

Two plus two equals four.

Keep your eye on the ball.

If you can't say anything nice, don't say anything at all.

Wipe your feet before you walk in the house.

Don't play with matches.

This game was about choices. What choices do you make? *Pause for responses.* You make choices every day—choices about who your friends will be, choices about what you will say or not say, and choices about whether you will pay attention in school or obey what your parents tell you. Often there's more than one right answer: You need to *know* that your eye should be on the ball; you have to *stop* looking at things other than the ball; you need to *do* something—keep your eye on the ball. "Know," "stop," "change," and "do" work together to help you make good choices.

Second Chronicles 34 talks about a boy named Josiah who made great choices. Josiah became king of Judah when he was just eight years old. That's pretty young for a king, but Josiah started off right by deciding to follow God. Before Josiah became king, the people of Judah had stopped following God. They worshipped idols, and they lost God's Word. Josiah got rid of all the idols. The Temple of the Lord had been destroyed, so he gave people the job of fixing God's house, and that's where they found a book containing God's Word. Josiah read it and then he read it to the people. He promised to follow God and to obey God's commands.

 Open your Bible to 2 Timothy 3:16-17, and show the page to the children. Second Timothy 3:16-17 says, **"All Scripture is God-breathed and is useful for teaching, rebuking, correcting and training in righteousness, so that the man of God may be thoroughly equipped for every good work."**

This passage uses some pretty big words, but we already know what they mean. Teaching means the things you should "know." *As you speak, do the motions that correspond with "know," "stop," "change," and "do," and encourage children to do them with you.* Rebuking means "stop." Correcting means you need to "change." And training in righteousness means the things you need to "do" to follow God. If you read the Bible and allow it to show you what you should know, stop, change, or do, you can make great choices just like Josiah. Let's pray.

 Dear God, thank you for giving us your Word to help us know how to live. Help us to read the Bible and learn how to make good choices in our lives. In Jesus' name, amen.

Daniel's Friends Are Safe in the Fiery Furnace

Bible Story: Daniel 3:1-30

 Bible Verse: "Be on your guard; stand firm in the faith; be men of courage; be strong" (1 Corinthians 16:13).

Simple Supplies: *You'll need a Bible, a handful of play money or real money, a toy, a bag from a fast-food restaurant, and a picture of a famous person.*

A long time ago, a king made a gold statue. He wanted people to worship the statue. When you worship something, you give it the highest value and you think of it first before anything else. This king told his people to bow to the statue every time they were near it. *Have everyone bow low.* If they didn't worship it, they would be thrown into a fire! *Have everyone say, "Ouch!"* Well, three men named Shadrach, Meshach, and Abednego stood up for God and said, "No way. We won't bow to a statue. It's fake. We worship God no matter what! God is real." *Have everyone stand straight and tall and say, "Worship God no matter what!" and then sit back down.*

Now we don't bow to gold statues, but we might forget God sometimes because other things seem more important to us. I'm going to show you some things people might think of before God. Each time I show you something, I'd like you to stand up straight and tall and say, "Worship God no matter what," and then sit back down. *Bring out a handful of play money and pause for kids to respond. Do the same with a toy, a bag from a fast-food restaurant, and a picture of a famous person.*

Good job standing up for God! Now let's return to our Bible story. The king was mad at Shadrach, Meshach, and Abednego because they worshipped God no matter what. The king threw them into a fire. But you know what? God protected them, and they didn't get burned. In fact, they didn't even smell like smoke!

Open your Bible to 1 Corinthians 16:13, and show the page to the children. First Corinthians 16:13 says, **"Be on your guard; stand firm in the faith; be** **men of courage; be strong."** Shadrach, Meshach, and Abednego were strong and courageous. They stood firm in the faith and we can too. Can you think of times in your life that you may need to stand up for God? *Pause for children's responses.* What can you do when you're faced with those situations? *Pause.* We can ask God to help us stand strong and keep us safe, just as he kept Shadrach, Meshach, and Abednego safe in the fire.

Let's say a prayer asking God to help us stand firm. Dear God, help us not to place other things before you. We know money, food, toys, or other people are nothing compared to you. Help us stand firm in the faith and be strong like Shadrach, Meshach, and Abednego. In Jesus' name, amen.

One at a time, have kids stand up and say, "Worship God no matter what" before they leave.

God Protects Daniel in the Lions' Den

Bible Story: Daniel 6:1-23

> **Bible Verse:** "Do not be anxious about anything, but in every-thing, by prayer and petition, with thanksgiving, present your requests to God. And the peace of God, which transcends all understanding, will guard your hearts and your minds in Christ Jesus" (Philippians 4:6-7).

Simple Supplies: *You'll need a Bible.*

What is the scariest thing about lions? *Pause for children to answer.* How would you feel if you were alone with a lion and couldn't get away? *Pause.* It would be pretty scary. Lions can be very mean, and lions play an important role in our Bible story today.

Our story today is about Daniel. *Open your Bible to Daniel 6:1-23, and show the passage to the children.* The king, Darius, had put Daniel in charge of one third of his men. There were two other men in charge of the rest of King Darius' men.

Because Daniel was so good at what he did, the king put him in charge of a whole kingdom. What are you good at? Choose a partner and tell him or her one thing you're really good at. *Pause to allow children to discuss.* Now tell your partner about one thing someone else does really well. This could be a friend, a family member, or someone famous. *Pause to allow children to discuss.* Good! There are lots of things that people can do well; Daniel's great gift was leadership. This made the other leaders jealous. They tried to find reasons to accuse Daniel and make him look bad, but they couldn't find anything.

Then these men came up with a plan. They knew Daniel loved God and wor-shipped God. They knew Daniel prayed every day. So these men went to King Darius and convinced him to make a law saying that no one should pray to any god or man except him, the king, for the next thirty days. Anyone found dis-obeying the law would be thrown into the lions' den. The king thought it sounded like a good idea, so he made the law.

Now Daniel continued to worship and pray to God. What are some ways you worship? *Have kids share ways they worship. For example, they may sing, play an instrument, or go to church. After kids have shared, have them share about times they pray, such as before a meal, at night before bed, or in the morning when they wake up.*

What do you think the men thought when they saw Daniel praying and wor-shipping God after he had been told not to? *Pause.* When the men saw Daniel, they went and told the king and said that Daniel should be thrown in the lions' den.

The king was upset because he knew he couldn't change the law, but he also didn't want to throw Daniel into the lions' den. He tried everything he could think of, but he just couldn't think of a way to stop this. So he had to do what the men asked and throw Daniel into the lions' den.

The king told Daniel, "May your God, whom you serve continually, rescue you!" *Open your Bible to Philippians 4:6-7, and show the page to the children.* Philippians 4:6-7 says, **"Do not be anxious about anything, but in everything, by prayer and petition, with thanksgiving, present your requests to God. And the peace of God, which transcends all understanding, will guard your hearts and your minds in Christ Jesus."** How can this verse help you when you face a hard time?

Well, Daniel sure faced a hard time. Daniel was thrown into a den, a pit where the lions lived. Then a stone was placed over the mouth of the den, and the king sealed it. Daniel was in there alone with the lions.

Tell kids to close their eyes and cover their eyes with their hands. Imagine you are all alone in a dark place. A stone covers the only exit to the room you are in. You know there are lions nearby. You hear the sound of lions' paws walking across the room toward you. You hear the sound of low rumbling growls. Then *(pause)* it's very quiet—all—night—long.

Have kids open their eyes.

The king was so upset about having to put Daniel in the lions' den that he didn't eat or sleep all night long. The next morning, the king went to the lions' den and called out, "Daniel, servant of the living God, has your God, whom you serve continually, been able to rescue you from the lions?" *Pause for several seconds allowing children to become a little bit anxious.*

What do you think the king heard? *Pause.* Daniel answered the king, telling him, "O King, live forever! My God sent his angel, and he shut the mouths of the lions. They have not hurt me, because I was found innocent in his sight. Nor have I ever done any wrong before you, O king."

The king had Daniel lifted out of the lions' den, and they didn't find any kind of wounds on him at all. Daniel had trusted God and God protected him. Do you think Daniel trusted God when he was in there with the lions? *Pause.* Daniel did trust God, and God protected him in a miraculous way! And you know what? God will protect you, too! You just need to trust him! Let's pray.

Dear Lord, thank you so much that you protect us in so many different ways! Help us to always remember what you did for Daniel and that you will protect us, too. Help us to always trust you in every situation. In Jesus' name, amen.

God Promises to Restore Israel After the Exile

Bible Story: Jeremiah 29:4-14

> **Bible Verse:** " 'For I know the plans I have for you,' declares the Lord, 'plans to prosper you and not to harm you, plans to give you hope and a future' " (Jeremiah 29:11).

Simple Supplies: *You'll need a Bible, a brown paper bag, a gift bag, and a box of crackers. Place the box of crackers in the gift bag and then place the gift bag inside the grocery bag.*

Bring out the brown paper bag and show it to the kids. God's special people—the Israelites—had not listened to God and done what he wanted. So for a long time they had to leave their homeland and live in a faraway place. It was a sad, dreary, blah, down time for the people. Kind of like this bag—blah, nothing much to feel good about. When have you felt sad or down? *Pause for children to respond.* Well, God didn't want his special people to continue to feel sad, down, and blah. God sent a man named Jeremiah to tell the people to "hang in there" through the sad times because God promised good things for them in the future. *Reach in the grocery bag and pull out a brightly colored gift bag.* I know what's in this gift bag, and it's filled with good things. If you only wait and trust, you'll know all about the good things in the bag.

Open your Bible to Jeremiah 29:11, and show the page to the children. Jeremiah 29:11 says, " **'For I know the plans I have for you,' declares the Lord, 'plans to prosper you and not to harm you, plans to give you hope and a future.' "** This verse tells us that we can trust that God has good plans for us. *Pause after each of the following questions and allow time for children to respond.* What do you think you'll do later today? What are your plans for tomorrow? next week? How about in one year? *Go around to several children and ask them how old they are now and then add ten years.* [Child's name], you are [number] years old now, and in ten years, you'll be [number] years old. What do you think you'll be doing when you're [number] years old? *Pause for children to share all kinds of plans.* Those are all wonderful plans. One thing we can count on is that God knows his plans for us, good plans that will give us hope and a future.

Let's thank God for the good plans he has for us. Dear God, thank you that you have good plans for us. Help us trust you through the bad times and know that all will be well. Thanks for loving us always. In Jesus' name, amen.

Reach in the bag and give kids the crackers. As they eat their snacks, tell them to remember that God has good plans for them.

Nehemiah Seeks God's Forgiveness for Israel

Bible Story: Nehemiah 1:1–2:9

> **Bible Verse:** "If my people, who are called by my name, will humble themselves and pray and seek my face and turn from their wicked ways, then will I hear from heaven and will forgive their sin and will heal their land" (2 Chronicles 7:14).

Simple Supplies: *You'll need a Bible and a cross in a stand.*

Let's try something before we start. Everyone stand and face me. *Pause while children do this.* Now everyone turn away from me. *Pause while children do this.* OK, now everyone face me again and sit down. *Pause while children do this.* What do you think it means to turn away from God? *Pause for children to respond.* When we turn away from God, we forget him and don't do what he wants us to do. God's special people—the Israelites—had turned away from God and forgotten him. *Have kids turn away from you.* So for awhile they had to leave their home and live in a faraway land. A man named Nehemiah turned to God, prayed, and said he was sorry. *Have kids face you again.* After Nehemiah turned to God and said he was sorry, God chose him to lead God's people back to their homeland.

Open your Bible to 2 Chronicles 7:14, and show the page to the children. Second Chronicles 7:14 says, **"If my people, who are called by my name, will humble themselves and pray and seek my face and turn from their wicked ways, then will I hear from heaven and will forgive their sin and will heal their land."**

Let's have this cross stand for God and all he's done for us. *Place the cross in the midst of the children.* It was wrong for the Israelites to turn away from God and forget him. Think of something wrong that you've done. Have you forgotten God? Have you forgotten to treat your family well? When you think of it, turn away from the cross. *Pause while you and the kids do this.*

Now, let's turn back to the cross and pray to God, telling him we're sorry for what we've done wrong. *Turn back to the cross and join hands for prayer.* Dear God, please forgive us when we turn away from you and forget to do what's right. Help us remember you and look to you for how to live our lives. In Jesus' name, amen.

When we turn to God, pray to him, and ask for his forgiveness, God hears us and forgives us and restores us. We feel better! *Have everyone wrap their arms around each other in a group hug.*

Nehemiah Rebuilds the Wall

Bible Story: Nehemiah 2:11–6:19

> Bible Verse: "Whatever you do, work at it with all your heart, as working for the Lord, not for men" (Colossians 3:23).

Simple Supplies: *You'll need a Bible, blocks, and a whistle.*

Help children to form small groups of three or four, and give each group a bunch of blocks. Appoint one person in each group to be the Knocker.

When I say "go!" I want you to start building with your blocks. Build quickly, because every time I blow this whistle, the Knocker has one chance to knock some blocks over. Even if your blocks fall, keep building until I tell you to stop.

Say "go!" and let groups build. Blow the whistle at random, maybe every ten to twenty seconds. After a minute or two, ask groups to stop and admire their creations.

I bet it was pretty frustrating to try to build when your blocks kept getting knocked over. Did you ever feel like you wanted to stop building? Why or why not? *Pause for responses.* Unfortunately, life can be hard work. And you'll meet too many people who want to knock over your work. Just when you think you've got it together—whether it's a friendship, a school project, or a big weekend you've planned—someone or something can come along and tap on it, causing some blocks to fall. It can make you feel like you just want to give up.

In the Bible, the book of Nehemiah tells a story of a guy who experienced a situation just like this. We pretended to build walls, but Nehemiah actually wanted to build a wall. The walls of Jerusalem had been destroyed, and Nehemiah wanted to give honor to God by rebuilding them.

Nehemiah organized the people to each rebuild a section, so that working together, they would have the walls built quickly. Then the Knockers came. *Walk between the children's buildings and, each time you mention opposition, knock over a block or two.* First outsiders made fun of their efforts to rebuild the walls. Next the outsiders plotted against them to stop the building. Then the workers who were building the wall got tired, and the work seemed too hard. The outsiders threatened to attack, and the Jews became afraid. People began to run out of food, and other Jews took advantage of them. The outsiders tried to trick Nehemiah, and they used Jewish prophets to try to trap him.

Nehemiah had a lot of problems trying to get the walls built. I imagine he might have felt like giving up. He might have felt like he couldn't deal with one more problem. Still, he never gave up.

Open your Bible to Colossians 3:23, and show the page to the children. Colossians 3:23 says, **"Whatever you do, work at it with all your heart, as working for the Lord, not for men."**

Nehemiah knew that God wanted the walls of Jerusalem to be strong to protect his people. If Nehemiah had tried to please people, he might have given up. The work really was too hard! But Nehemiah wanted to please God, so he worked with all his heart at getting the walls rebuilt.

Finally the people finished building the walls. And you know what? Those pesky outsiders who kept trying to interfere became afraid. They realized that God had helped the Jews to rebuild their walls.

What are some things you try to do in your own life that seem too hard for you to do? *Pause for children's responses.* How can you be like Nehemiah in those situations? *Pause for children's responses.*

Let's pray together. Dear God, thank you that we can work for you and not give up. Help us to remember that we can do everything in our lives for your glory. In Jesus' name, amen.

Encourage children to remember Nehemiah's persistence each time they see a "wall" this week.

Esther Saves Her People
Bible Story: Esther 2-9

> **Bible Verse: "For we are God's workmanship, created in Christ Jesus to do good works, which God prepared in advance for us to do" (Ephesians 2:10).**

Simple Supplies: *You'll need a Bible, and a piece of modeling dough for each child.*

I'm looking for things that are useful, and I'll bet you can help me. *Point to an obvious example in your meeting room, such as a podium or a clock, and then explain the use of that item.* Look around the room, and when you see something useful, point at it and freeze. *Point at the item you just explained and freeze to show children what you mean.* I'll come around and unfreeze you, and then you can tell me what you see that's useful and what it does.

You can choose to unfreeze every child, or just choose a few to represent the whole. Either way, be sure to thank everyone.

You've pointed to some very useful items. But did you realize that you were useful to me just now? I asked for help, and you helped me. What else do you do to help others? *Pause for responses.* How can others help you? *Pause.*

The Bible tells a story about a helpful woman named Esther. She helped to save all the Israelites living in Persia from being killed. *Give each child a small piece of modeling dough.* I'll tell you the story of Esther and you play with modeling dough while you listen. When the story's done, you can share with us what you made if you like.

Many of the Jews had been taken away from their homes and forced to live in another country. Esther's uncle Mordecai was among those Jews. Esther's parents had died, so Mordecai raised her like a daughter.

The king of Persia chose Esther as his queen. One of the high officials of the land, a guy named Haman, didn't like Mordecai. When he found out that Mordecai was Jewish, Haman hatched a plot to destroy all the Jews. No one knew, however, that Esther was also Jewish.

Have you ever done something really scary? *Pause for responses.* When Mordecai found out about Haman's plot, he asked Esther to go to the king on behalf of her people. That may not sound scary, but if someone approached the king without his invitation and he didn't want to see the person, he or she could be killed. Esther found herself in a bind: If she didn't go to the king, Haman's plot meant she would die along with the Jews; if she went to the king and he didn't want to see her, she might also die. Pretty scary.

Esther told Mordecai about her scary situation, but he told her that God might have allowed her to be queen just so that she could help the Jews in this particular situation. So Esther risked her life to help her people.

God honored Esther's willingness to be used by him. The king invited Esther into his presence when she appeared in his court, and he granted her any wish. Eventually, she told him that she was Jewish and that Haman had ordered all Jews to be killed. The king got very angry. He got rid of Haman, and invited Mordecai to take Haman's place as his high official. And the Jews did not die because of Haman's scheme.

Allow children who want to share their modeling dough creations to do so. Follow up with questions about the usefulness of what they made. For example, if someone sculpted a flower, ask how that flower might be useful.

You used modeling dough to create some beautiful things. God used Esther to save the Jews from Haman's plot, and God can use you to do good things too.

Open your Bible to Ephesians 2:10, and show the page to the children. Ephesians 2:10 says, **"For we are God's workmanship, created in Christ Jesus to do good works, which God prepared in advance for us to do."**

God made each of you to do good things, and he has prepared good works for you to do. Like Esther, God might want you to do some things in your life that seem scary. But if you continue to do the good works God has prepared, he will take care of you as he took care of Esther. Let's pray together.

Dear God, thank you for preparing good things for us to do. Give us the courage to do those good things. In Jesus' name, amen.

Encourage children to take their modeling-dough creations with them.

Job Remains faithful in Suffering

Bible Story: Job 1:1-2:10; 42:1-6, 10-17

> **Bible Verse:** "But those who hope in the Lord will renew their strength. They will soar on wings like eagles; they will run and not grow weary, they will walk and not be faint" (Isaiah 40:31).

Simple Supplies: *You'll need a Bible, animal crackers, small drinking cups, and sheets of red dot stickers. Recruit a volunteer to take children's cups away from them at the appropriate time, and to add twelve more animal crackers to each cup.*

Who knows people who love God and always try to do what God wants them to do? *Pause for children to respond.* Our Bible story today is about a man named Job. He is described as being "blameless and upright; he feared God and shunned evil." What do you think "shunned" means? *Pause for children to answer.* If you shun something, it means that you stay away from it. So Job stayed away from bad things. He was a man who wanted to do what was right, what God wanted him to do.

God had blessed Job with many wonderful things. He had a big family. In fact, he had seven sons and three daughters! How many of you come from a big family? What's it like to have that many people around all the time? *Pause.*

Job also had a lot of animals. We're going to take a little inventory of what Job had. *Give each child a small drinking cup.* Job had seven thousand sheep. *Give each child seven animal crackers, but tell them not to eat them yet.* Job had three thousand camels. *Give children three more animal crackers.* And Job had hundreds of oxen and donkeys. *Give children two more animal crackers.* Now that's a lot of animals! Well, on top of all of that, Job had many servants to help him. God had really blessed him. *Remind children to hold on to their animal crackers and not eat them yet.*

How do you think Satan feels about people like Job? *Pause.* Satan gets really jealous that someone would want to obey God instead of him. So he gets mad. What do you think Satan would want to do with people like Job? *Pause.*

In our Bible story today, we'll find out what Satan does to try to get Job to turn away from God. Let's take a look at it. *Open your Bible to Job 1:1-2:10, and show the passage to the children.*

Satan told God that Job had no reason to complain because he had a wonderful life. He had family, friends, servants, and livestock. Why should Job turn away from God? Satan said that if Job were to lose everything, he would curse God. In other words, Satan thought that Job wouldn't remain faithful to God if he lost everything he had. So God told Satan that he could take anything he wanted away from Job, but he couldn't hurt him.

What do you think Satan did to Job? *Pause for children to answer.* Satan took away almost everything Job had. He took away his children and he took away his livestock. *Have the volunteer take away the cups from the children.*

What do you think Job's response was? *Pause.* Let's look at what the Bible says. *Read Job 1:21-22 aloud.* Job didn't blame God at all! Job knew that it was the Lord who gave him everything to begin with, and it was the Lord's right to take it away. So Job praised God. How many of you feel like praising God when something you want is taken away from you, as your animal crackers were taken away? *Pause.* It's hard, isn't it? Well, let's continue to see what else happens to Job.

Satan was still mad. Job was still faithful to God. Satan told God that if he allowed him to hurt Job's body, then Job would blame God. So God told Satan he could hurt Job, but he couldn't kill him.

So Satan caused Job to have very painful sores all over his body from his feet to the top of his head. *Pass around the sheets of red dot stickers to each child. Have children place red dots on their faces, hands, and arms.* I want you to pretend that these red dots are sores on your body. Can you imagine what it would be like to have real sores all over your body, like Job had? I want you to show me what you think it would be like to walk with painful sores on the bottom of your feet. *Have kids stand and demonstrate what it would be like to walk with sores on the bottom of their feet. After a few moments, have kids sit down again.* You only have pretend sores, but Job had real sores and they were very painful. Job's wife and friends told him to curse God and die to end his suffering. But even as he sat in a pile of ashes and scraped his sores, he wouldn't do what Satan wanted him to do—curse God. *Have kids scrape off the dots and ask a volunteer to collect them.* Job continued to trust God.

When Satan was finally through making Job suffer, what do you think Job did? *Pause. Open your Bible to Job 42:1-6, 10-17 and show the passage to the kids.* Job prayed for his friends and God heard him. Then God gave back to Job even more than he had before! All Job's brothers and sisters and anyone who knew him before came to his house and comforted him. And each person gave Job a piece of silver and a gold ring. Then the Lord blessed the last part of Job's life even more than the first part. *Have your volunteer redistribute the cups with twice as many animal crackers to the children.* At the end of his life, Job had thousands of animals, including sheep, camels, oxen, and donkeys—plus seven sons and three daughters. And Job lived another 140 years!

God made a promise that he will help us in hard times too. Let's take a look at our Bible verse for today and see what that promise is. *Open your Bible to Isaiah 40:31, and read the verse aloud.* Isaiah 40:31 says, **"But those who hope in the Lord will renew their strength. They will soar on wings like eagles; they will run and not grow weary, they will walk and not be faint."** God promises that if we put our hope and our trust in him, as Job did, he will help us. Let's pray together.

Dear Lord, thank you for always being there for us even when things are hard. Help us to be like Job when we go through hard times and always be faithful to you and trust you. In Jesus' name, amen.

Allow children to eat their crackers.

Scripture Index